De Havilland Mosquito

An Illustrated History

Stuart Howe

Foreword by Group Captain John Cunningham, CBE, DSO**, DFC*, AE, DL

Crécy Publishing Limited

First published in 1992 by Aston Publications Limited

Revised edition published in 1999 by Crécy Publishing Limited
Reprinted 2006

A CIP record for this book is available from the British Library

Printed in England by The Amadeus Press

ISBN 0 947554 76 9   9 780947 554767

Front cover illustrations:
Background: An interior view of the FB.VI's cockpit showing the P8 compass, throttle quadrant and,
behind the control column grip, the elevator trim tab. BAe; Cutaway drawing: An FB.VI; Lower: B.IV
DZ637, seen here, was one of 20 converted to carry the 4,000lb bomb. This particular aircraft was the
first to drop one operationally on 23 February 1944 over Dusseldorf. On that operation it was flown
by Flt Lt McKeard of No. 692 Squadron; Centre (flying): B.IV DZ313 on an early test flight from
Hatfield in 1942. BAe.
Back cover:
Mosquito B35, C.A.F. Harlington, Texas, October 1973.

Crécy Publishing Limited
1a Ringway Trading Estate, Shadowmoss Road, Manchester M22 5LH
www.crecy.co.uk

Contents

Foreword

By
Group Captain John Cunningham, CBE, DSO**, DFC*, AE, DL

The Mosquito was without doubt the most versatile and useful aircraft of the 2nd World War. That its successes became legendary is a tribute not only to its air and ground crews, but to de Havilland and the skills of wood-workers in Britain, Canada and Australia.

For two and a half years I flew the night-fighter version of the Mosquito. Its handling qualities were delightful and the performance far superior to any other similar aircraft of the period and, as a test pilot for de Havilland after the war, I was fortunate to fly many other versions of the Mosquito.

Stuart is well known for his work in the field of Mosquito preservation and in this book, his third on the subject, he presents the full story of this superb aircraft using many rare and never seen before photographs, covering all aspects of the Mosquito's design, development and operational career. The Mosquito has a unique place in aviation history.

Foreword to New Edition

When Crécy Publishing approached me with the idea of reprinting *The de Havilland Mosquito: An Illustrated History*, I persuaded them to add nearly 60 more photographs. It wasn't feasible to insert most of these within the original chapters, so the next best thing was to insert a section at the back of the book. I hope that this meets with your approval.

In addition to those kind people who appear in the photo credits, I would like to thank for their help: Harry Ellis, Doug Morrison, W.M. (Max) Garroway, Peter Nock, P. M. Froom, Peter Kempe, E. J. Davies, Peter Jolly, Robert M. Stitt, Richard A. Franks and finally to my lovely wife Barbara for her support and patience.

Lastly, I am still looking for further Mosquito photographs, in any form or guise, for possible use in any future books on this fabulous aircraft. Many thanks.

Stuart Howe
September 1998

Group Captain John Cunningham with Sir Douglas Bader to his
left in front of the prototype Mosquito, W4050, in the early 1960s.

This NF.XIX, seen on its delivery flight, was the third of its type to be delivered to the Swedish Air Force and served with the FT Wing at Västeras. This Mosquito (which was formerly TA281) crashed in May 1949 (via *Peter Kempe*)

G-AJZE (ex-RG231) seen here at Cranfield in 1948 was one of two PR.34s that were used by the BEA Gust Research Unit for research into clear air turbulence. (*British Airways*)

Introduction

Looking back at the history of aviation there are a number of aircraft types which stand out above all others, both in their design and their achievements. Without any doubt, high on the list is the de Havilland Mosquito, one of the truly great aircraft of all time.

All right, I may be somewhat biased towards the Mosquito, but what other aircraft before or since has matched its versatility and record of service? Almost 50 different versions of the Mosquito were produced and in all of these it excelled, whether it was as a pure bomber, fighter-bomber, day and night fighter, or as a photo-reconnaissance aircraft. In the more passive role it was used to carry passengers and mail and to tow targets for the ground, sea and air forces. In civil hands it was used for surveying, mapping and private use as well as for experimental work and pylon racing. It was even modified with folding wings for use on aircraft carriers! That the Mosquito appeared at all was only due to the determination of Geoffrey de Havilland, who fought against official policy and thinking to have his project recognized. As a nation we are fortunate to have had men such as him, especially in times of conflict.

In this book I have not attempted to relate the full history and operational record of the Mosquito as this has already been well documented in several fine books already, but as a believer in that a picture can tell a thousand words I have presented the story of the Mosquito pictorially, with detailed captions. I have collected Mosquito photographs from private and official sources over many years and my idea for this book is to present photographs which have not been published before. However, there *are* some which have been seen before as they are classic shots and simply cannot be substituted. The wartime use of the Mosquito has been well covered photographically, so I have included the equally fascinating use of the Mosquito by overseas air forces and civilian users. It is also about time that the Royal Navy had its own chapter as so little has been published on this subject in the past. I shall be most grateful for any further information concerning the aircraft shown in this book, and for any photographs that readers may care to let me borrow for copying for possible use in any future editions.

My own interest in the Mosquito goes back as far as I can remember. My mother, Isabel, made electrical conduits for the Mosquito in rooms rented by de Havilland above Nicholson's at Fleetville in St. Albans, while my father, Sidney, was in the stores of the Mosquito Repair Organisation at Hatfield. I also lived underneath the flight paths to Hatfield and Leavesden, which helped deepen my interest in the Mosquito, as did nearly 20 years of looking after the three Mosquitoes of the Mosquito Aircraft Museum. This then is my small contribution to over 50 years of Mosquito history.

I would like to thank the following for their invaluable assistance with this book: R. W. Edwards, Mike Hooks, Ray C. Sturtivant, Norman Malayney, Rudy Binnemans, Peter Kempe, Milan Micesvski, Bojan Dimitrijevic, J. J. Petit, Bjorn Olsen, Jim D. Oughton, E. J. Davies and all those kind people whose names are credited with their photographs in this book. Special thanks also to Babs, my wife, for her assistance and encouragement. Also invaluable as sources of information and reference are: British Aerospace, Hatfield, Royal Air Force Museum, Hendon, and the following books: *The De Havilland Mosquito* by M. J. Hardy (David and Charles); *Mosquito* by J. Martin Sharp and Michael Bowyer (Faber & Faber); *The Aircraft of 100 Group* by Martin Streetly (Robert Hale); *Mosquito Squadrons of the Royal Air Force* by Chaz Bowyer (Ian Allan); and *Roundel*, published bi-monthly by the British Aviation Research Group.

Stuart Howe

Dedication: To my mother Isabel

Construction

With one or two exceptions, de Havilland's pre-war designs had been aimed at the civil markets of the world and it was as a direct result of World War II that the Mosquito came into being.

Design work on the Mosquito commenced in late 1938 when the design team moved to Salisbury Hall, an 18th-century moated manor house a few miles away from the company's headquarters at Hatfield. The idea was to get on with the design unhindered by officialdom and away from the main factory, which was in danger of being bombed. The design team was led by R. E. Bishop and the design itself, until then given only the design number DH98, soon became known as the Mosquito. Thanks mainly to Sir Wilfred Freeman, the Air Member for Development and Production at the Air Ministry, and at that time virtually de Havilland's only ally in the Government, a contract for 50 Mosquitoes was awarded to de Havilland on 1 March, 1940, even though the detail construction had yet to be started.

At a time when most manufacturers were constructing metal aircraft, de Havilland used wood for the construction of the Mosquito. Besides greater performance because of its lightness, there were a number of other advantages in using wood, not the least being to cut down the initial design stages and to enable the prototype to be constructed rapidly, as a result of which the aircraft was put into production very quickly. From the time design work started until the Mosquito entered squadron service was less than two years, a quite remarkable achievement. The use of wood also avoided additional strains on the supply of metal and skilled labour and made full use of the available skills of the woodworking industry, including the employment of many coachbuilding and furniture factories as sub-contractors.

The prototype Mosquito, W4050, was constructed at Salisbury Hall, and when it was completed it was taken by road to Hatfield, where it made its maiden flight on 25 November, 1940. Three more Mosquitoes were constructed at Salisbury Hall before production moved to Hatfield.

Once the Mosquito had proved its worth, Hatfield could not cope with the increased demand, so de Havilland's factory at Leavesden went over to Mosquito production, soon to be followed by Standard Motors at Coventry, Percival Aircraft at Luton and, later, Airspeed at Portsmouth. After the war a production line was also set up at de Havilland's Hawarden, Chester, factory. Before the end of 1942 a production line had been set up in Canada at de Havilland's Downsview factory near Toronto and in 1944 in Australia, in the company's Bankstown, Sydney, factory. A total of 7781 Mosquitoes of all marks was built, when production ended in 1950: 6535 in Britain, 1034 in Canada and 212 in Australia.

The prototype Mosquito undergoing assembly at Salisbury Hall in October, 1940, after which it was dismantled and taken to Hatfield for its first flight. Just behind the tail is the Mosquito mock-up which helped finalize the design.

A Mosquito bomber in the making. Here, the inner skin and the between-skin structural members were being fitted in slots on the mahogany mould. In the next stage the balsa wood filling was fitted. This had the purpose of stabilizing the thin inner and outer skins and was fitted between the structural members in strips. The strips were then cemented on to the inner skin and, as can be seen on the fuselage half behind, flexible steel-band cramps were used to give the required pressure for bonding. The balsa was then surface smoothed to the contours of the fuselage, after which the outer skin panels were fitted and cemented into place. The skins were made from 1.5 and 2mm three-ply birch. *(British Aerospace)*.

Before the two fuselage halves are cemented together, over 60 per cent of the internal equipment was installed and this resulted a large saving in assembly time. The trunnion mounting for the wing attachment pick-ups is seen in the centre. *(British Aerospace)*.

A general view of the fuselage assembly hall at Downsview, with fuselage halves and whole fuselages in various stages of completion. *(National Museum of Science & Technology)*.

The operation of joining the halves of the fuselage together was known as 'boxing-up'. Aft of the wing gap, the fuselage halves were cramped together using laminated wooden bands, seen here being tightened on a Mosquito at the Downsview assembly plant at Toronto in Canada. *(National Museum of Science & Technology)*.

The wing of the Mosquito was made in one piece with a front and rear spar and stressed skin covering. Here, rear spar assemblies are under construction, possibly at Parker Knoll, High Wycombe. *(British Aerospace)*.

The top surface of the wing was made up of two birch plywood skins, interspaced by square section stringers which ran the length of the wing. On the undersurface the outboard panels embodied only one plywood skin, while the centre section of the wing (which housed the fuel tanks) was made up of stressed balsa-plywood panels forming the tank doors. Both main spars were of box construction separated by interspar ribs made of spruce laminations. Wings are seen here under construction at Wm Birch's factory at High Wycombe in August 1943. Note the large sign at the far end of the hall 'WHATEVER YOU DO DON''T SPARE THE GLUE'. *(British Aerospace)*.

In the foreground and to the left are semi-completed wings, while in the centre wing skins are being made up on jigs, with a batch of rear spar assemblies in the background. *(British Aerospace)*.

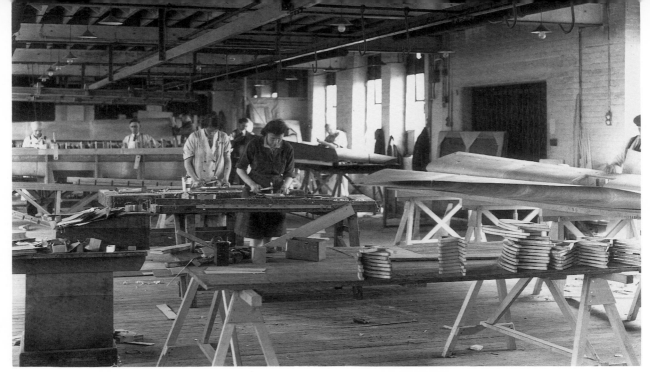

The moulded wing leading edges were made up from laminated plywood strips and were attached outboard of each engine and tapered towards the wing tip. Here they are being constructed, while in the foreground the ladies are making up the leading edge nose ribs. Note the piles of finished ribs. *(British Aerospace)*.

In this picture rudders are under construction. The Mosquito's rudder was of all-metal construction, covered in fabric. The cut-out at the rear of the rudder is for the trim tab. *(British Aerospace)*.

The completed wing is here being fitted out with its engine controls and wiring, with the fuel tanks also being fitted into the wing's four tank bays. The undercarriage assemblies and engine bearer pick-ups have also been attached. *(British Aerospace)*.

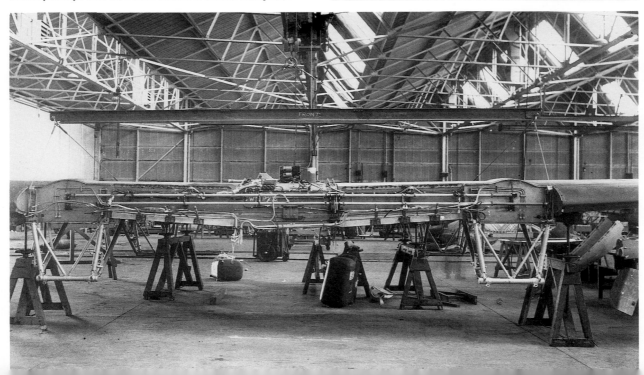

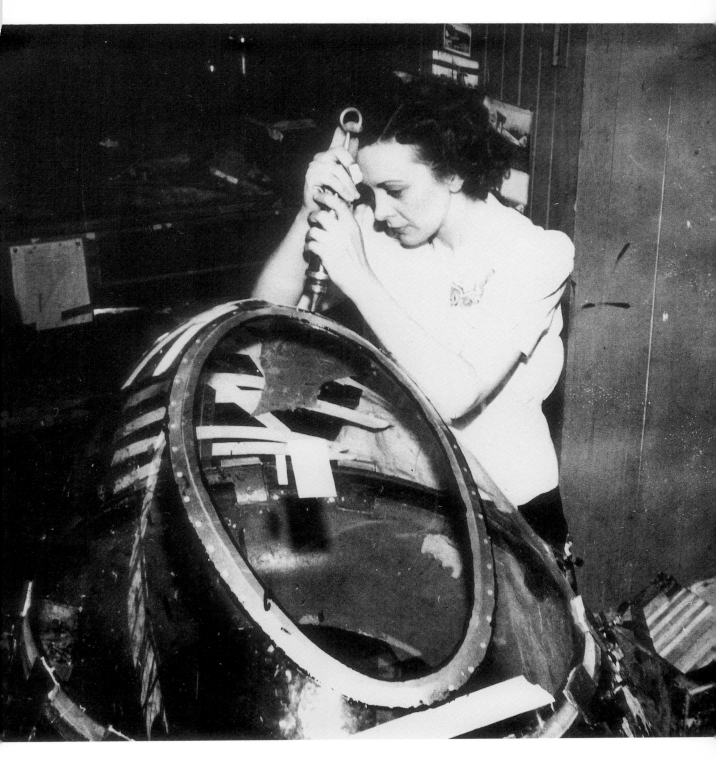

The Perspex nose-cone of a bomber Mosquito was made in two pieces. Here, sealant is being applied to the edges of the metal band which attaches the glass clear view panel to the moulded Perspex nose-cone. *(National Museum of Science & Technology.)*

Canadian workers are seen here putting radiator assemblies together. The oil coolers, glycol and cabin heater radiators are built up into a single block and assembled as a unit in the leading edge of the wing, between the fuselage and engine on each side. *(National Museum of Science & Technology.)*

A posed shot, but nevertheless an indication of the paperwork involved during the construction of the fuselage. Inspectors were on hand throughout construction and assembly, and items inspected bore their own official stamp of approval. *(National Museum of Science & Technology.)*

The production of the first Canadian Mosquito went on in great secrecy in Bay 3 at Downsview; this photograph was the first ever taken of a Canadian Mosquito by photographer Joe Holliday, who edited DH Canada's magazine *Mosquito.* The Mosquito is here in final assembly, in company with Ansons, which were also built at Downsview at that time. *(National Museum of Science & Technology.)*

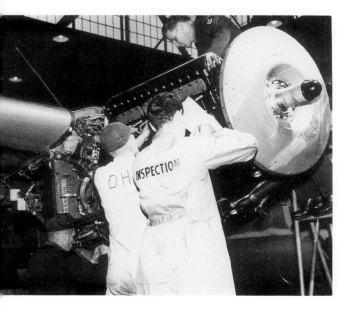

With RCAF personnel looking on, a DH Canada engine fitter and inspector complete the installation of a Mosquito's starboard Merlin engine at Downsview. *(National Museum of Science & Technology.)*

The completed cockpit of a bomber Mosquito at Downsview.
(National Museum of Science & Technology.)

About to leave the factory is the last fuselage, that of an NF. 38, to be finished at Lebus at Tottenham Hale. The driver is Maurice Grace, who worked for Wades Transport. Lebus was one of many sub-contractors in and around the London area, ranging from the large furniture and vehicle manufacturers, to small joinery and engineering works. *(via Joan Spencer.)*

An FB.VI fuselage in the Dope Shop at Standard Motors factory at Ansty, Coventry; the red dope was applied by brush. Before the camouflage paint was sprayed on, a final coat of silver dope was applied to keep out the ultraviolet rays of the sun. The cellulose dope could also be sprayed on.

FB.VIs on the final assembly line at Hatfield. Note the fuselage shells in the middle of the two lines.

FB.40s on the Bankstown assembly line in Australia. A52-12 in the foreground crashed on a pre-delivery test flight due to wing flutter at high speeds. A modification to the wing was then made to all Australian-built Mosquitoes.

FIG. 2.

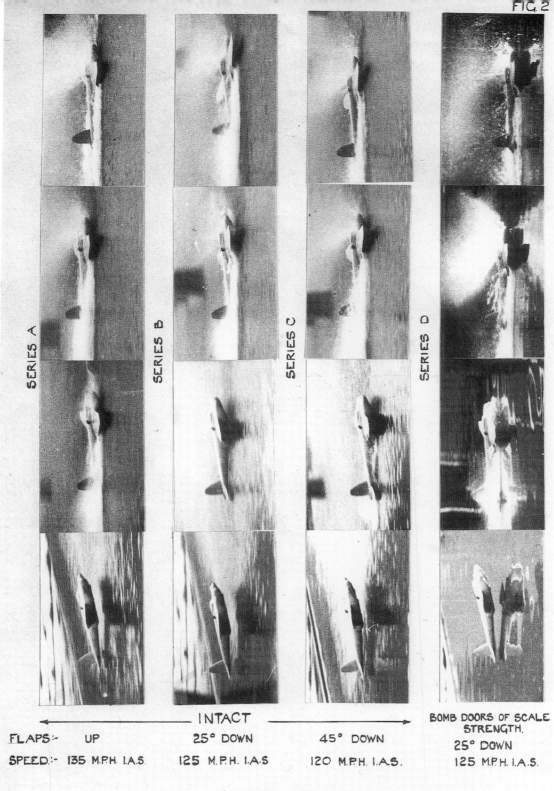

SERIES A   SERIES B   SERIES C   SERIES D

|←——————————— INTACT ———————————→| | BOMB DOORS OF SCALE STRENGTH. |

FLAPS:-   UP   25° DOWN   45° DOWN   25° DOWN

SPEED:-   135 M.P.H. I.A.S.   125 M.P.H. I.A.S.   120 M.P.H. I.A.S.   125 M.P.H. I.A.S.

MOSQUITO

WEIGHT AT DITCHING:- 17,000 LBS. INTERVAL BETWEEN SUCCESSIVE PHOTOGRAPHS = ½ SEC. FULL SCALE.

To test the Mosquito's ability to make an emergency landing on water, ditching trials were carried out at the A&AEE at Boscombe Down using an exact scale model. This photograph depicts a series of four separate ditchings with a ½-second interval between each frame. In series 'A' the flaps are up with a speed of 135 mph IAS, while in 'B' the flaps are 25 degrees down at 125 mph IAS. In 'C' the flaps are 45 degrees down at 120 mph IAS, while in 'D' the bomb doors are tested with the flaps 25 degrees down at 125 mph IAS. The scale weight of the model at ditching was 17,000 lb. *(A&AEE.)*

In this photograph taken on the 30 August, 1944, the port tailplane and elevator are seen mounted on a rig in the wind tunnel at the A&AEE. Like all other aircraft, the Mosquito had its share of structural failures and handling problems, and wind tunnel tests such as this one were carried out to determine the cause. *(A&AEE.)*

Two shots of the Mosquito Aircraft Museum's B.35 taken early
in 1990 towards the end of its ten-year restoration. The
Mosquito's radiators, tank doors, engine firewalls and
undercarriage doors have still to be fitted, as have the canopy
glazing and nose cone. TA634 was duly completed in time to
celebrate the Mosquito's 50th Anniversary on 25 November,
1990, at Salisbury Hall and was finished in the markings of
No.571 Squadron. The wing of TA634 was constructed by
Education Supplies Association at their Stevenage factory,
hence the lettering 'MK 35 E.S.A.', which the restoration team
found stencilled on the front spar web when they removed the
starboard radiator for refurbishing. The lettering was re-applied
and can just be seen in the photograph. *(Stuart Howe.)*

Taken in the summer of 1985, this photograph shows the author doping fabric strips around the dinghy hatch cut-out behind the cockpit of TA634, an area which even when in service was liable to water seepage, and care had always to be taken to waterproof the compartment. Standing in the cockpit is Ian Thirsk, doping fabric strips to the edges of the cockpit cut-out, while in the foreground is the dinghy box itself.

Showing further detail of the Mosquito's construction is this shot of the author doping a fabric patch to the nose of FB.VI TA122 early in 1979. TA122 was delivered to No 605 Squadron at Coxyide in Belgium early in April 1945 and saw at least one operational sortie before hostilities ended. It soon after took up communication duties, but by August 1945 was on the strength of No 4 Squadron and was still with the squadron at Celle when it was SOC on 30 June, 1950. It was then sold to Delft Technical University as an instructional airframe. The fuselage of TA122 was eventually put into storage with the RNLAF Museum, from where the author arranged its donation to the MAM; TA122 arrived at Salisbury Hall on 26 February, 1978. The author decided to retain the original fabric, but this had been removed around the nose to show the construction, hence the insertion of the fabric patches. By this time the cockpit's interior had been removed for restoration. During removal the author found two spent bullet cases in the nose. *(Stuart Howe)*.

In 1980 the remains of a TR.33, thought to be either TS449 or TW233, were donated to the MAM from Israel with the main component consisting of the one-piece wing, which is seen here in the museum's workshops during an early stage of its restoration. MAM members Colin Ewer and Chris Rowe are here discussing the newly refitted rib 4 on the port wing with Ian Rumney looking on. This wing is one of the pre-production examples of the TR.33 with a fixed wing, for subsequent production aircraft incorporated a folding mechanism for use on aircraft carriers. *(Stuart Howe.)*

The Mosquito's birthplace, Salisbury Hall, and the Mosquito Aircraft Museum framed through the front quarter window of Mosquito T.III RR299 in July 1984 by the author. *(Stuart Howe.)*

Bombers

Bomber Command received its first Mosquito on 15 November, 1941, when Geoffrey de Havilland delivered W4064 to No. 105 Squadron at Swanton Morley. The squadron spent the next six months working up on the Mosquito and showed great enthusiasm in its new mounts, an enthusiasm not yet shared by many of Bomber Command's high-ranking officers, who had yet to be convinced of the concept of an unarmed bomber. The chance to put into action the theories and lessons learnt in months of practice came in the early hours of 31 May, 1942, when Sqn. Ldr. Oakeshott took off in B.IV W4072 for Cologne with a bomb load of 1500 lb, followed an hour and a half later by Plt. Offs Kennard and Johnson in W4064.

The Mosquito's career as an offensive weapon had begun, and although losses in the early daylight raids were quite high, its successes mounted with daring daylight raids such as the first to Berlin on 19 September and the precision low-level attack on the Gestapo HQ in Oslo on 25 September. The little wooden bomber soon endeared itself to its crews, who found that it could outrun the enemy fighters that were sent up to intercept it and that the airframe could take a tremendous amount of punishment and still get home.

Daylight operations ended on 1 June, 1943, when all bomber variants were transferred to No. 8 Bomber Group, Pathfinder Force and their new tasks were high-level nuisance raids and, flying OBOE-equipped Mosquitoes, target marking for the heavy bombers. At night the Mosquito came into its own and it achieved the lowest loss rate of an aircraft operated by Bomber Command throughout the war, some 0.63 per cent. A total of 39,795 sorties was flown and 26,867 tons of bombs were delivered. Not at all bad for an unarmed bomber.

After the prototype, the first bomber version of the Mosquito was known as the B.IV Series i and was a conversion of the PR.I. Only nine were so converted and were able to carry a bomb load of 2000 lb.

The first true production Mosquito bomber flew in March 1942, designated the B.IV Series ii, serving as a day and night bomber; BOAC used a number for the night-time runs to Sweden, while others served in the PR role. Power was provided by a pair of Rolls-Royce Merlin 21s or 23s of 1460 hp. The Mk VII was the Canadian equivalent of the B.IV, but was only used in North America.

The B.IX had two-stage Merlins and some were converted to carry the 4000 lb bomb; it was a B.IX, LR503 of No. 105 Squadron, that flew more operational sorties than any other Mosquito, a total of 213. However, perhaps the most significant of the bomber versions was the B.XVI, which first flew in January 1944 and was constructed from the outset to carry the 4000 lb bomb; two 100-gallon drop tanks, one under each wing, could also be carried, giving a still-air range of 1470 miles and a speed of 419 mph.

The B.XX and B.25 were Canadian versions of the B.IV Series ii that were used extensively by the RAF in Europe, while the ultimate bomber was the British-built B.35, powered by Merlin 113A/114A engines; almost all B.35s served after the war and a number were later converted to target tug standards (TT.35) and served until 1963 in this role. Others were converted to PR. 35s, a number of which were sold to civilian users at home and abroad. No fewer than 12 B/TT.35s survive today.

The scene from the cockpit of B.XX KB267 'E' of No. 627 Squadron, taxiing out at Woodhall Spa on 18 August, 1944, on its way to drop markers on the turning point to target the flying bomb depot at L'Isle Adam, north of Paris, crewed by Flg. Off. J. F. Thomson, DFC (RNZAF), and Flg. Off. Brian E. B. Harris, DFC.

Carrying the Master Bomber, KB267 crashed in Holland near the town of Steenbergen on 19 September after completing a successful attack on München Gladbach. On board was Wg. Cdr. G. P. Gibson, VC, and his navigator Sqn. Ldr. J.B. Warick, DFC. Their loss was a great blow to Bomber Command. Beyond the Mosquito being readied for its next sortie is High Park Farmhouse, a familiar landmark for the squadron's crews. *(B. E. B. Harris)*

From his seat the navigator sees this view of his Mk XIV bombsight in the cramped nose of this No. 627 Squadron Mosquito. The bombsight was not used when the Squadron operated from Woodhall Spa on low-level marking, the pilot releasing his markers via a button on his control column. *(B. E. B. Harris.)*

The crew bus about to unload the crew for 'S' DZ525 at Woodhall Spa. The dispersal pan in the foreground is that of 'B' Flight next to the perimeter track. A B.IV, DZ525 was delivered to No. 109 Squadron in March 1943, the squadron being part of the Pathfinder Force and the first to be equipped with OBOE, which was a very accurate radar bombing aid. The squadron made their first OBOE sortie on 20 December, 1942, when six Mosquitoes attacked a coking plant at Lutterade in Holland. In March 1944, DZ525 was transferred to No. 692 Squadron at Gravely, which was part of No. 8 (PFF) Group's Light Night Striking Force. Not long after it was damaged and after repair was flown to Marshalls at Cambridge for modifications. It then joined No. 627 Squadron, No. 5 Group's sole Mosquito unit, which operated as a marker unit for the Group's Lancasters. This long-lived Mosquito was eventually damaged on 14 September, 1945, but was re-categorized as a write-off a week later. *(B. E. B. Harris.)*

Standing in front of 'M' of No. 627 Squadron are Plt. Off. J. G. D. Platts and his navigator C. G. Thompson (RCAF). This Mosquito, DZ521, was a survivor of 110 operational sorties, although only a small number of these had been with No. 627 Squadron.

This crew crash-landed on 29 June, 1944, whilst attacking a flying bomb depot at Beauvoir in 'P' DZ482. Platts was wounded and became a PoW, but Thompson evaded capture and was back on the squadron within a few weeks. *(B. E. B. Harris.)*

The nose-art on DZ415 'Q' of No. 627 Squadron is sporting only 7 ops, but the stout fellow in the bowler looks keen to add another! The road sign behind the figure says 'Berlin'. *(B. E. B. Harris.)*

Members of the ground crew of 'B' Flight of No. 627 Squadron at Woodhall Spa in 1944 carrying out a 'DI' (Daily Inspection) on B.IV DZ615, which had originally served with No. 139 Squadron. The B.IV carried a 2000 lb bomb load, although a small number were converted to carry a 4000 lb bomb load, which, even with a reduced maximum fuel capacity of 497 gallons, still gave a maximum operational radius of 535 miles. *(B. E. B. Harris.)*

Flt. Lt. John Burt and Flt. Lt. Ronald Curtis of No. 109
Squadron at Little Staughton stand in front of their Mosquito
B.IX ML907 with their ground crew after completing
the aircraft's 100th operational sortie late in 1944.
(Roy W. Edwards.)

An early production B.IV, DK300 was delivered to No. 109
Squadron at Stradishall to have special radar installed on 21
July, 1942, the following month moving to Wyton, where the
squadron received eight more B.IVs, which were used for
OBOE trials. Gp. Capt. D. C. T. Bennett was in overall
command to develop this radar, which would hopefully make
accurate night bombing possible. In this picture one of the
ground crew is giving DK300's starboard undercarriage some
attention. *(MAP.)*

A trio of B.35s of No. 139 (Jamaica) Squadron at Hemswell in May 1950 awaiting permission from the control caravan to take off. Note the large-size code letters with the two outside Mosquitoes in an overall silver colour scheme with red spinners, while the middle aircraft still retains its wartime colour scheme of matt black under-surface and camouflage top surfaces. Earlier with G-H and later H2S installed in their Mosquitoes, No. 139 Squadron led the other Mosquito squadrons of the Light Night Striking Force to their targets. By the end of the war the LNSF (including three squadrons from No. 8 Group) flew some 26,255 sorties for the loss of 108 aircraft. A remarkable achievement considering that 68 percent of its operations took place when the heavy bombers were not operating.

TK620, in the foreground of the picture, was laid down as an NF.30, but was completed as a B.35 and was eventually scrapped in February 1957. In the middle, VP194 spent its active life with No. 139 Squadron until sold to D. Bushal Ltd for scrap in March 1955. Making up the trio is VP185, which spent most of its time with the squadron until it was involved in a flying accident and Struck Off Charge on 20 July, 1950. *(via M. J. Hooks.)*

The bomber Mosquito in this photograph taken on 30
September, 1943, was damaged in a belly landing and the nose
had to be cut open in order to take the crew out. The RAF
returned the aircraft to Hatfield to be taken apart for spares, but
de Havilland's Mosquito Repair Organization thought
otherwise and the repaired Mosquito was later returned to
service. This type of repair was not uncommon and the MRO
also sent out working parties to repair Mosquitoes at their
operational airfields. Damaged wings were simply sawn off and
new extensions were butt-jointed on. Some of the original
hangars that were used by the MRO can still be seen at Hatfield
today. *(British Aerospace.)*

Another view of the above aircraft taken at a later stage. The balsa has been laid over the inner ply skin and once the glue had set the outer skin was then attached. In the background the leading edge of the tailplane is under repair, while beyond this is the wing, which has been completely stripped down. *(British Aerospace.)*

B.35 TK605 in an undignified pose at Langham in the mid-1950s after its port undercarriage had collapsed. In this wintry scene the undercarriage can be seen lying by the port tailplane. TK605 was delivered into store from Hatfield with No. 22 MU in December 1945 until it was delivered to Brooklands Aviation at Sywell in October 1951 for conversion to target-towing standards. After a spell with No. 22 MU again, it was flown to No. 2 Civilian Anti-Aircraft Co-operation Unit at Langham on 15 July, 1953, with whom it remained until SOC on 28 February, 1957. *(Kenneth H. Jackson.)*

A fine shot of B.IX LR500 at Hatfield shortly after leaving the production line. It was delivered to No. 109 Squadron at Wyton in May 1943, but later the same month was transferred to No. 105 Squadron at Marham. The squadron had been engaged on daylight sorties, but July saw it come under the control of No. 8 Group PFF. LR500 had already been fitted with OBOE when it joined the squadron. Later in 1943 the squadron commenced particularly daring and accurate precision bombing sorties against pinpoint targets in western Germany. LR500 suffered some damage in November 1944 which was deemed repairable by a contractor's working party, but eventually it was re-categorized 'E' (complete write-off) on 30 May, 1945, and was scrapped. *(RAF Museum.)*

A B.XVI of No. 128 Squadron having probably slewed off the runway into the rough ground, causing the undercarriage to fold back. The photograph was possibly taken early in 1945, when the squadron was based at Wyton.

Hatfield-built B.35 TA669 was delivered into store in May 1945 and remained there until 30 September, 1953, when it was flown to Brooklands Aviation at Sywell for TT conversion. It was eventually issued to the 2nd Tactical Air Force for use at the Armament Practice Station at Sylt in West Germany, where it was SOC on 30 November, 1956. *(P. A. Cooke.)*

B.XX KB123 is pictured here on 15 May, 1945, after suffering hail damage – see the pock-marked spinner and the holes in the wing leading edge. Judging by the state of the rear nacelle and the bent-back propeller the unfortunate KB123 must have suffered the collapse of the port undercarriage. From Canada KB123 was flown across the Atlantic to Prestwick, where it was prepared for RAF use by Scottish Aviation Ltd and was delivered to No. 608 Squadron at Downham Market on 5 September, 1944, but later that month was transferred to No. 1655 Mosquito Training Unit at Warboys (later becoming No. 16 Operational Training Unit). Because of the hail damage KB123 was declared a write-off.

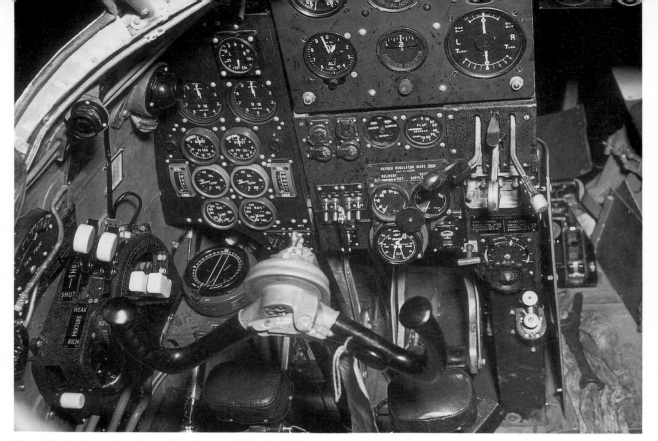

The 'office' of a bomber Mosquito taken on 27 March, 1943,
at Hatfield in the final stages of being fitted out.

Armourers winching a 4000 lb 'Cookie' into the bomb bay of a
B.XVI of the Light Night Striking Force.

TK656 was the last B.35 to be built at Hatfield and is seen here on 10 April, 1946, being towed out with some ceremony. After first going to Marshalls for modifications it was issued to No. 14 Squadron at Wahn in November 1947. Not long after it went into store with No. 19 MU and after some further work, this time at de Havilland it eventually arrived at Manby in November 1951, followed two weeks later by a move to Benson and No. 58 Squadron, where it helped in the squadron's task of the aerial photo survey of Britain. TK656 was eventually sold to Lowton Metals at Leigh near Warrington on 16 January, 1957. *(British Aerospace.)*

A wintry scene at de Havilland Canada's Downsview factory with B.XXV KB428 outside its servicing tent. Some 343 B.XXVs were delivered to the UK, although KB428 does not appear to have been one of them. *(G. A. Jenks Collection.)*

After leaving the factory, B.35 RS719 joined the Empire Test Pilots' School at Cranfield in September 1946, but was damaged in May 1947 and repaired on site by No. 71 MU. In 1950 it was loaned to Airspeed's and after a period in store it was issued to No. 3 CAACU. February 1957 saw it again in store with No. 27 MU at Shawbury before it was issued to RAF Woodvale on 16 April, 1947, joining the Met Flight there. Finally it went to No. 5 CAACU on 31 January, 1958, and in May it suffered repairable damage, but was SOC a month later. The target-towing gear is clearly seen in this photograph of RS719. *(via R. C. Sturtivant.)*

Percival-built at Luton, B.XVI PF498 was delivered to RAF Defford in March 1945, and did not join No. 627 Squadron at Woodhall Spa until August, little more than a month before it was transferred to the Bomber Development Unit at Feltwell. December 1946 saw PF498 training crews with No. 16 OTU at Cottesmore, followed by spells with Nos. 139 and 109 Squadrons until October 1948, when it was delivered to RAF Kirkham to become Instructional Airframe number 6607M. PF498 is seen here at the Central Bombing Establishment at Marham. Note the H2S radar dome under the fuselage. PF498 was then allocated to a Civil Defence Unit at Chorley, Lancashire, surviving long enough for the wing to be rescued by Tony Agar who is rebuilding a Mosquito at the Yorkshire Air Museum. *(Jim D. Oughton.)*

B.35 TJ138 is here being reassembled by an RAF team at Colerne with the fuselage being lowered on to the wing. Slings have been attached to a spacer bar at the front and rear of the fuselage to prevent the fuselage from breaking at its weakest part, just behind the cockpit canopy. TJ138's first unit was No. 98 Squadron at Celle, but not for long, as re-equipment plans made TJ138 redundant and it was flown back to the UK. After storage and conversion to TT its next unit was No. 5 CAACU at Woodvale, coded 'Z'. The aircraft was retired early, for on 15 June, 1959, it was sent to No. 27 MU and then in July was handed over to No. 71 NU at Bicester, where it was given the instructional airframe number 7607M and was used for exhibition purposes. TJ138 was later transferred to the RAF Museum and was housed at Colerne, Finningley and then Swinderby. It has undergone a complete refurbishment at St. Athan and is displayed in the Bomber Command Hall at the RAF Museum, Hendon, where it arrived early in 1992.

A B.IV delivering a Highball weapon during trials. The intention was to use them against ships and experiments were also made against tunnels. The idea was that these weapons would be released a mile from the target, bounce over any obstructions, hit the side of the ship, sink and explode. No. 618 Squadron worked up on the weapon, but in the end it was not used in case the idea was copied by the enemy.
(British Aerospace.)

A wintry scene showing B.IX ML901 in March 1946, at Farnborough, where it was delivered after manufacture and remained there on trials work until SOC on 15 May, 1947. Note the large tube-like affair poking through the Perspex nose and what appears to be an air vent in the side window – connected perhaps with the 40 lb rockets installed under the wings, a fitment which the bomber version of the Mosquito did not normally carry. *(RAE Farnborough.)*

A fine shot with everything down of B.35 G-MOSI (RS709) about to land at Blackbushe on 3 June, 1984. After a varied and interesting career which included target towing with No. 3 CAACU, and as a film star in *633 Squadron* and *Mosquito Squadron* it made two trips to the USA, the last as the property of the USAF Museum at Dayton, Ohio, where it resides today in the colours and markings representative of the PR.XVIs used by the USAAF in Europe during the war. *(R. J. Kenward.)*

B.IV DK338 over the Hertfordshire countryside in September 1942. *(RAF Museum/Charles E. Brown.)*

B.IV DZ515 joined No. 139 Squadron in March 1943, where it joined in the unit's activities over occupied Europe but very soon suffered some damage. It was back on strength by the end of April. Not long after DZ515 was lost and was officially listed as missing on 15 July, 1943. Note a ground crew member by each engine with his hand on the primer pump waiting for the pilot to start the engine. Once the engines were started he would pull the chocks from under the wheels.

B.IV or B.XX with the serial number A518, a number which does not tie up with an active aircraft, so it must be an instructional airframe, possibly in Canada but maybe even Australia or New Zealand. *(MAP.)*

Fighters

The first Mosquito fighter squadrons to be formed were No. 157 Squadron at Debden, commanded by Wg. Cdr. Gordon Slade, and No. 151 Squadron at Colerne, both with NF.IIs. After working up on the Mosquitoes, the first operational patrol was flown by Flg. Off. Graham-Little and Flt. Sgt. Walters of No. 157 Squadron on 27 April, 1942, to intercept enemy aircraft attacking Norwich.

By June 1943 there were 12 Mosquito-equipped squadrons defending Britain by night, although some daylight patrols were also flown; on D-Day some of the Mosquito fighter squadrons patrolled over the Normandy beachhead, six in all forming part of No. 85 Group, TAF, and from March 1944 until the end of the war 299 enemy aircraft had been claimed as destroyed by them. Mosquitoes were again in the forefront when the V-1 flying bombs were launched against Britain and in total they destroyed some 623 of these weapons, many of them at night.

By the end of 1942 Bomber Command was losing an ever-increasing number of heavy bombers to enemy night-fighters and in the Mosquito it saw a long-range fighter capable of escorting bombers all the way to their targets, so No. 100 Group was formed in November 1943 to organise night-fighter protection of Bomber Command. The Mosquitoes not only flew with the bombers to their targets but stayed with them over the target and on the way home as well. Other Mosquitoes patrolled over the enemy night-fighters' airfields and intercepted any that were taking off or landing; later on in the war the night-fighter Mosquitoes also carried bombs under their wings as well as incendiaries and napalm when they attacked the enemy airfields.

The first fighter version was the F.II, which flew for the first time in May 1941 and was used as both a day and night-fighter (the latter equipped with AI radar); this version was also employed for intruder work with Fighter and Coastal Commands and it was not until January 1944 that the F.II was finally replaced. The NF.XII was a night-fighter conversion of the F.II and was equipped with AI Mk. VIII radar in a thimble nose in place of the four machine guns. This mark first flew in August 1942 and was powered by Merlin 21s or 23s.

Next came the NF.XIII – with a wing similar to the FB.VI - able to carry underwing drop tanks or bombs and having a still-air range of 1260 miles and a maximum speed of 394 mph. The top-scoring Mosquito was probably NF.XIII MM466, which served with Nos. 488 and 409 Squadrons and in all claimed 11 victories. The NF.XV followed, which was a high-altitude fighter with two-stage Merlins. The NF.XVIII was equipped with the more advanced SCR720/729 or AI Mk 10 radar and was followed by the NF.XIX, which had a similar specification. A development of the NF.XIX was the NF.30, with two-stage Merlins, a maximum speed of 424 mph and an operational ceiling of 35,000 ft. Post-war the NF.36 served with the RAF until 1953, while the last version, the NF.38, saw no frontline service, although many were sold abroad.

Used extensively throughout the war and after was a dual-control version of the F.II, the unarmed T.III (although at least one overseas Air Force did in fact arm some of their's). The Canadian versions were known as the T.22, T.27 and T.29, and Australia built the T.43 – all had Packard-built Merlins.

Leavesden-built NF.30 NT306 entered service with No. 151 Squadron on 11 January, 1945. Part of 100 Group, the squadron defended Britain's skies at night and in 1918 it was the RAF's first night intruder squadron to be formed. NT306's career ended on 11 September, 1946, when it was written off during a single-engine landing at Odiham from which the crew escaped unhurt. The 'G' after the serial number indicated that the aircraft was carrying special or secret equipment and had to be guarded at all times. *(RAF Museum.)*

A picture of a trials aircraft fitted with nose-mounted ASV (air-to-surface-vessel) radar. *(via R. C. Sturtivant.)*

NF.XIII HK428 was delivered to No. 29 Squadron at Ford in January 1944 and shot down a Ju 88 on 17 June, 1944. In October it was badly damaged, and after repair by de Havilland was sent to the Central Gunnery School at Carfoss. It was eventually SOC on 16 September, 1946. The thimble nose contains Airborne Interception Radar (AI) Mk VIII. This radar was developed by the Telecommunications Research Establishment (TRE) and built by Ekco and GEC, entering service in 1942. AI Mk VIII had a wavelength of 10cm and a frequency in the region of 3 GHz and had a maximum range of 6½ miles.

HK360 came off the Leavesden production lines as a NF.II, but was flown to Marshalls at Cambridge for the fitting of SCR 720 radar and became an NF.XVII. SCR 720 (British designation AI Mk X) was developed by the Radiation Laboratory, Massachusetts Institute of Technology and built by the Western Electric Company and the radar entered RAF service in 1943. AI Mk X had a wavelength of 10cm with a range of 8 to 10 miles. HK360 was one of the first NF.XVIIs to enter service with No. 456 Squadron at Fairwood Common in January 1944, a squadron then in the forefront of Britain's night defences. On 17 April it joined the Fighter Interception Unit at Ford, which used Mosquitoes for test purposes and operational trials, and eventually HK360 was SOC as obsolete on 31 January, 1946. HK360 is here being flown by Flg. Offs. Desmond Tull and Peter Cowgill. In the month after this photo was taken this crew shot down eight enemy aircraft over Germany, then went missing. Here HK360 accompanies captured Me 410 TF209 (10259), which was used for comparison trials with the Mosquito, crewed here by Sqn. Ldr J. H. Williams and Flg. Off. F. J. MacRae. *(Jeremy Howard-Williams.)*

In August 1942 Ju 86Ps started flying over Britain at heights of up to 41,000 ft and dropped their bombs at will, immune from the Spitfires that attempted to intercept them. The answer was the Mosquito. MP469 was constructed as the prototype pressure cabin bomber and within a week the experimental shop at Hatfield had converted the bomber by fitting a fighter nose and substantially lightening the airframe, and on 15 September MP469 reached a height of 43,500 ft and was the answer to the Ju 86P. The following day it was flown to Northolt by Flg. Off. Sparrow to join the High Altitude Flight of Fighter Command, but the call to intercept a raider did not come. In November the aircraft was fitted with AI Mk VIII radar in the nose and the four machine guns were installed in a blister under the fuselage. After radar trials at Defford, MP469 joined the FIU on 4 February, 1943, but less than three weeks later it was with No. 85 Squadron at Hunsdon for operational trials, the squadron then being under the command of Wg. Cdr. John Cunningham. The high-altitude fighter became known as the Mk XV and four more joined MP469 at Hunsdon, although MP469 reached the highest altitude of 44,600 ft. In August it flew north to RAF Turnhouse to await the possibilities of raiders over Scotland. This remarkable aircraft ended its days as instructional airframe No. 4882M with the School of Aeronautical Engineering at Henlow. *(British Aerospace.)*

NF.30 MV529 is here being made ready for test flights at Leavesden in September 1944, from where it was delivered to No. 218 MU for installation of its AI Mk X radar and then went on to active service with No. 25 Squadron at Castle Camps, which was engaged in the air defence of Great Britain, and was particularly successful against the air-launched V-1s carried by He 111s off the east coast. On 23 January, 1945 MV529 was destroyed in a mid-air collision over Camps Hall in Cambridgeshire while on a practice interception with another Mosquito. *(British Aerospace.)*

NF. 30 MM813 undergoing routine servicing at Wittering in 1946. The NF.30 was fitted with two-stage Merlins and it could operate at a maximum speed of 424 mph at 26,500 ft, and the still-air range at recommended cruising speed was 1180 miles. The NF.30 could also carry two under-wing tanks or two 250 lb bombs. *(Eddy Gosling.)*

VT654 was one of a batch of 50 NF.38s built at Hatfield and Chester, 21 of which were delivered to Yugoslavia, VT654 being one of them. The NF.38 was fitted with the later Merlin 114 engines and did not see front-line squadron use. NF.38 VX916, completed at Chester in November 1950, was the 7781st and last Mosquito to be built, and this too was delivered to Yugoslavia. *(MAP.)*

In this picture the trolley-ack is attached to NF.36 RL123 of No. 25 Squadron at West Malling in the spring of 1950, ready for the day's practice sortie. RL123 first entered service with No. 29 Squadron on the same airfield on 22 August, 1946, but in October moved across to No. 25 Squadron and remained with the unit until it went away for modifications in June 1950. After suffering serious damage it was repaired at Brooklands Aviation, Sywell, following which it was prepared for despatch to the Middle East where it arrived on 16 July, 1952, and it joined No. 39 Squadron at Kabrit in Egypt. At Kabrit No. 219 Squadron was also equipped with Mosquitoes and these two units were the only night-fighter squadrons in the Middle East zone. RL123 was back in the UK by March 1953 and this long-lived Mosquito was eventually sold as scrap to J. Thompson Ltd on 16 October, 1954. *(MAP.)*

Awaiting permission to taxi is F.II DZ700 of 'B' Flight, No. 333 (Norwegian) Squadron at Leuchars in 1943. DZ700 started its career with No. 235 Squadron in April 1943 and besides service with No. 333 (Norwegian) Squadron, it also saw service with No. 248 Squadron and at several Operational Training Units before transferring to Royal Naval Air Station Arbroath on 29 March 1946. The F.II was a day and night long-range fighter and intruder. Later in the war many F.IIs were refurbished with new engines to extend their operational lives. *(via Cato Guhnfeldt.)*

An F.II of No. 307 (Polish) Squadron at their Exeter base in the autumn of 1942. This squadron was the first Polish night-fighter unit, flying Defiants and Beaufighters until they received their Mosquitoes in December 1942, working up on the later mark night-fighters until the squadron was disbanded on 2 January, 1947, with NF.30s. The F.II illustrated is probably being used for training purposes and the AI Mk IV receiving aerials on the front of the nose cone can clearly be seen. *(J. B. Cynk.)*

Another view of a No. 307 (Polish) Squadron F.II taken on 9 November, 1942, at Exeter, this time the mount of Capt. G. Ranoszek. Note the five kill symbols painted beneath the cockpit. *(J. B. Cynk.)*

NF.36 RL145 'H' of No. 141 Squadron about to land at its Coltishall base. The squadron's badge can just be made out on the Mosquito's fin, a not unusual practice on post-war aircraft. RL145 started its career with No. 264 Squadron in March 1946, this particular squadron going on to complete almost ten years of Mosquito operations. RL145 also saw service with No. 23 Squadron for a few months and was eventually sold as scrap to R. J. Coley & Son on 19 January, 1954. *(via Peter Hall.)*

Piloted by test pilot Pat Fillingham, T.III RR299 is about to land after a short demonstration flight at the Farnborough Air Show in September 1966. After service with No. 3 CAACU at Exeter, RR299 was acquired by Hawker Siddeley in July 1963. It was kept airworthy for 33 years but was tragically destroyed while performing in an Air Show at Barton on 21 July, 1996 with the loss of its crew, Ken Moorhouse and Steve Watson. *(Stuart Howe.)*

An unusual view showing test pilot George Ellis preparing for a display at Humberside Airport in July 1983 in RR299. Former bomber crews would know Humberside Airport by its earlier name of Kirmington. The T.III had a fighter control stick and dual controls and one or two overseas users did in fact put guns into their trainers. Two other T.IIIs survive today, TW117 moved to a new home with the Royal Norwegian Air Force Museum, while TV959 was taken down from the roof of the Imperial War Museum at South Lambeth, London and moved into storage at Duxford. Some thought has been given to eventually making it airworthy. *(Stuart Howe.)*

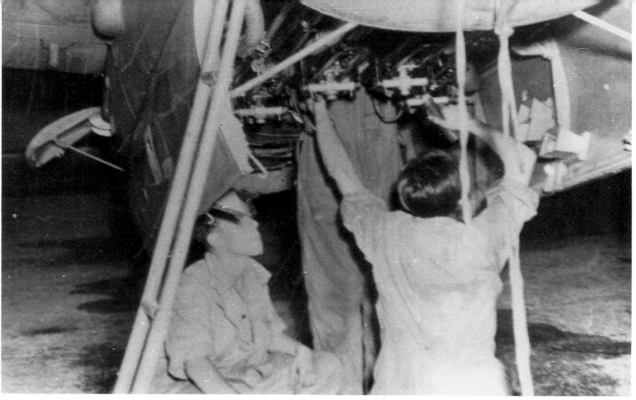

Armourer Joe Slater is here inspecting the rear gun mountings of the 20mm cannons installed in an NF.36 of No.39 Squadron at Fayid in Egypt, circa 1950. The 20mm cannons proved to be very reliable and in this picture the ejector chutes for the spent cartridge cases can be seen on the inside of the port gun bay door. Usually 300 rounds were carried. *(Joe Slater via D. M. Seager.)*

NF.XIX TA446 of No. 157 Squadron in a sorry looking state after a belly landing following engine failure at Shipdham, Norfolk, on 17 January, 1945. It was declared Category 'E' (complete write-off) the same day and was officially SOC on 26 January. TA446 had joined the squadron at Swannington in October 1944 after a brief stay with No. 85 Squadron on the same airfield, No. 157 Squadron became the first unit to operate the fighter Mosquito and became heavily involved in bomber support operations, although it spent several months during the summer of 1944 on anti-'Diver' operations against the V-1 flying bombs, claiming at least 20 destroyed. Back on BS operations, TA446 destroyed a Ju 188 on the night of 16/17 January, 1945, so could the accident possibly be a result of this action? *(Keith Goodchild.)*

RL248 started out as an NF.36, but was converted at Hatfield
with later Merlin engines and became the prototype NF.38.
It saw no squadron service, but was delivered for radar trials to
RAF Defford in September 1947, where it remained until
delivered into store with No. 27 MU at Shawbury in May 1952,
and was sold as scrap to Henry Bath Ltd at Kirkby on
30 September, 1954. *(Official US Air Force Photo.)*

The fighter prototype W4052 on an early test flight. W4052
made its first flight on 15 May, 1941, from Salisbury Hall in the
capable hands of Geoffrey de Havilland. After trials with the
A&AEE at Boscombe Down it joined the Fighter Interception
Unit at Ford and was eventually scrapped on 28 January, 1946.
(RAF Museum).

NF.XVII DZ659 was laid down at Hatfield as a F.II but was modified with a 'Universal' nose and fitted with SCR 720/729 'Eleanora' radar, also known as AI Mk 10. The aerial for the SCR 720 radar can be seen beneath the fuselage behind the cannon ports as can the azimuth aerials at each wing-tip. DZ659 was delivered to the FIU at Ford on 1 April, 1943, where it remained, apart from six months at Defford, and was eventually SOC as obsolete at No. 10 MU, Hullavington, on 28 January, 1946. *(via Jerry Scutts.)*

Another angle of NF.XIII HK428. The NF. XIII's maximum speed was 394 mph at 13,800 ft and it had an operational ceiling of 28,800 ft. *(RAF Museum.)*

The Canadian-built T.29 pictured here was a dual-control conversion of the FB.26 powered by Packard-built Merlin 225s, and very few were used in Europe. It is here being towed in after a test flight, most probably at DHC's Downsview factory in Toronto. *(National Museum of Science & Technology.)*

An impressive photograph of an NF.36 moving out for take-off,
and well used it looks too. Within the plastic radome can be
seen the AI Mk X scanner and aerial element. In peacetime the
radome was usually left unpainted. Underneath the access door
to the radome is the camera gun housing.

NF.36 RL243's first unit was the Central Flying Establishment at West Raynham in October 1945, and after four years it moved over to No. 23 Squadron on the same airfield. Here it developed rogue characteristics, which were sorted out by Brooklands Aviation. It then saw service with Nos 141 and 264 Squadrons and was finally sold as scrap on 16 October, 1954. *(via R. C. Sturtivant.)*

F.II DD723 briefly joined No. 85 Squadron in September 1942 at Hunsdon before suffering some damage. Soon after it was repaired it was delivered to the Rolls-Royce airfield at Hucknall in July 1943, where it was fitted with chin radiators for Lancaster power unit trials. It was returned to the RAF after overhaul by Marshalls at Cambridge in 1944. *(Barry Goodwin.)*

NF.30 MM695 of the Central Fighter Establishment at
Tangmere in the early summer of 1945. Previously it had
served with No. 219 Squadron at Hunsdon and ended its days
as instructional airframe, number 6381M with No. 1 Radio
School. The 'G' after the serial number indicated special
equipment fitted, which had to be guarded while on the
ground. The small 'T' antenna under the starboard wing
outboard of the engine nacelle is for the radio altimeter.
(Aviation Photo News)

NF.30 NT422 pictured here served with Nos. 29 and 609 Squadrons and was delivered to Halton as an instructional airframe, number 6674M, and it lingered on until the late 1950s along with a number of other NF.30s and PR.XVIs. Some remains were still extant on the airfield into the 1980s. *(J. M. Gradidge.)*

KA888 is a Canadian-produced T.27 which was based on the T.22, the Canadian version of the British T.III.

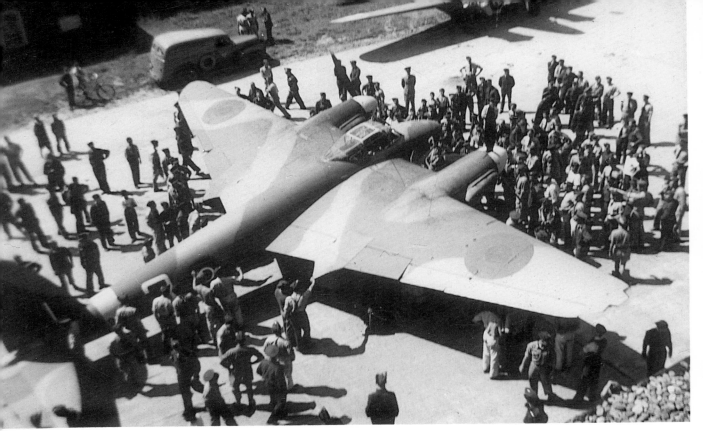

This Mosquito is obviously the centre of much interest at what is probably DHC's Downsview plant. The aircraft is a trainer, possibly the first T.III sent over from the UK to help train Canadian pilots on to the Mosquito. *(Lloyd Carbutt.)*

A line-up of NF.30s of No. 125 Squadron at Church Fenton in 1945.

A close-up of the 'Monica' tail warning radar installed in NF.30 MM747/G of No. 406 Squadron in the latter half of 1944, when the squadron was involved in Bomber Support duties over Europe. As well as a defensive device, 'Monica' sets were also used offensively with aircraft that were also equipped with AI Mk IV intercept radar. Code named 'Mahmoud', a single Mosquito would fly to one of the 22 known Luftwaffe night-fighter assembly points, the idea being to catch the enemy interceptors before they reached the bombers. The 'Mahmoud' Mosquito would offer itself as bait by flying straight and level until a contact was picked up astern. The Mosquito would then break to port or starboard and attempt to swing round behind the contact, transferring to the forward-looking AI Mk IV and then effect an interception. This manoevre was known as 'Whiting'. *(via G. Cruickshank.)*

NF.36 RL152 of No. 264 Squadron, probably taken at Linton-on-Ouse or Coltishall in the late 1940s or early 1950s. The squadron received its first Mosquito, W4086, on 3 May at Colerne and, except for a gap of five months, operated the type until February 1952. Note the multi-coloured spinners and also the length of material hanging from the rear of the undercarriage bay. This was attached to the undercarriage locking pin, which was inserted by the ground crew after each flight to avoid the inadvertent retraction of the undercarriage. The streamer was coloured red and acted as a visual indication that the locking pin was in place. The 'Monica' tail warning installation can also be seen underneath the tailcone. *(MAP.)*

F.II DZ754 of No. 333 (Norwegian) Squadron being refuelled
at Leuchars in June 1943. It was lost off the Norwegian coast
on the 23rd of the same month, *(via Tom Arheim.)*

Another shot of DZ754 taken in June 1943, just before it was lost. Here, a Norwegian airman paints the aircraft's identification letter 'F' Freddie on the Mosquito's fuselage. *(via Tom Arheim.)*

Fighter-Bombers

Of all the Mosquitoes built, the most widely used was the FB.VI, over 2700 of which were constructed. The FB.VI was the bomber and fighter versions combined and was operated as a day and night fighter-bomber, intruder and long-range fighter. When the FB.VI first started operational flying those enemy pilots who managed to catch such a Mosquito napping had an unpleasant surprise in store, for this mark fired back with an armoury of four .303 machine guns and four 20 mm cannon. Internally, later versions could carry two 500 lb bombs in addition to two more 500 lb bombs under the wings. Alternatively, four 60 lb rocket projectiles could be carried under each wing, or a combination of mines, depth charges or drop tanks.

The first operational FB.VI came off the line at Hatfield in February 1943 and the first squadron to be equipped was No. 418 Squadron at Ford, followed by Nos. 605 and 23 Squadrons. These Mosquitoes intruded deep into enemy territory and it was at night that they really came into their own, when they took over from the Allied long-range fighters and light bombers so that the enemy gained no respite and very soon came to fear the Mosquito and its deadly sting.

The FB.VI was also used to great effect by Coastal Command against enemy shipping and coastal targets off Norway and Europe, and an even more deadly version of the FB.VI was produced which, in place of the four 20mm cannon, carried a Molins 57mm (six-pounder) quick-firing cannon which could pump out 25 shells in as many seconds. Its purpose was to attack enemy submarines and 18 were built of which the first two were delivered to No. 248 Squadron at Predannack in October 1943.

Many FB.VIs also served in the Far East, operating from bases in India and Burma against Japanese targets. Canada and Australia both produced their own versions of the FB.VI – the Canadians the FB.21, later replaced by the FB.26, and the Australians the FB.40, which was used exclusively by the Royal Australian Air Force in the Far East. When the Canadian Mosquitoes first entered RAF service the ground crews had to adapt to US instrumentation and bolt sizes as well as non-standard equipment, but these problems were soon overcome.

A deck-landing version of the FB.VI was produced for the Royal Navy as the TR.33 and post-war numerous FB.VIs were exported to many different countries and gave excellent service, even after the new generation of jets had entered service.

One of the most famous of all Mosquito operations was the attack on Amiens Prison. Here, in tribute three FB.VIs with their bomb doors open fly low over the prison after the war.

A line-up of Australian-built FB.40s at No. 5 OTU Williamtown, NSW, in December 1944. Their overall colour scheme is foliage green and the Mosquito in the foreground, A52-35, was lost when it was abandoned by its crew and crashed 5 miles south of Morriset, NSW, on 15 February, 1945. Many FB.40s were converted to PR.40s. *(Frank F. Smith.)*

The scene at RNZAF Woodbourne in around 1956 when Mosquitoes were being scrapped after being sold as surplus. On the left next to an FB.VI is an Australian-built T.43 NZ2308, one of four purchased from Australia to help train RNZAF crews on to the FB.VI. NZ2308, ex-A52-1054 and A52-20 (it was reserialed when converted from FB.40 to T.43), was delivered to New Zealand on 13th June by Flt. Lts R. K. Walker and F. Whiteley. After its flying career came to an end with 479.35 hours on the airframe, it was put into storage at Woodbourne and was eventually one of the batch of 16 Mosquitoes offered by tender in June 1956. Fifteen of these were sold to the Ansa Orchard Equipment Company of Upper Moutere, Nelson.

Out of the 80 FB.VIs ordered from the UK all but four arrived safely, the 12,300 mile flight usually being completed in under two weeks with about 50 hours, flying time. Today, one complete FB.VI exists in New Zealand, NZ2336/TE910, which was bought at one of the surplus sales by John Smith of Mapua and he still has it at his home. The Ferrymead Aviation Society of Christchurch have the remains of NZ2328/TE758 and NZ2382/HR339 which they will eventually build into a complete machine, and Ted Packer, also of Christchurch, acquired many components from scrapped Mosquitoes which he has subsequently donated to the RNZAF Museum at Wigram. The museum has started to restore these with the intention of making up a complete example. To complete the preserved Mosquito scene in New Zealand, mention should be made of T.43 NZ2305/A52-1053 which is being restored by the Museum of Transport and technology at Western Springs, Auckland. *(Cliff Horrell.)*

Another view of the Mosquitoes being scrapped at
Woodbourne. Cliff Horrell bought a number of surplus aircraft
and thanks to him some major components survived, many of
which were acquired by Ted Packer, who recently donated his
collection to the RNZAF Museum where work is about to
commence on rebuilding a Mosquito for the museum. After the
engines and all useful components had been taken off, the
airframes were simply hauled to the nearby riverbed and burnt.
(Cliff Horrell.)

This FB.VI of No. 23 Squadron is fitted with 'ASH' radar in
place of its nose-mounted machine guns. 'ASH' was a fairly low-
level radar with a maximum range of 3.5 miles, minimum 600 ft
and it could also be used as a navigational aid. Also the 'ASH'
aircraft carried 'Gee', a navigational and blind bombing device,
and 'Monica', a tail warning radar, fitted to all 100 Group's
Mosquitoes. *(Eddy Gosling)*

A trio of FB.26s on a visit to Kapuskasing Airport in Ontario in
the later stages of the war, probably on a refuelling stop.
(Don Campbell.)

FB.VI PZ399 entered service with No. 305 (Polish) Squadron in November 1945 at Melsbroek and is pictured here over Holland. It later served with No. 107 Squadron at Guterslöh and was written off on 13 May, 1948. The 'Gee' whip aerial can be seen on the rear of the cockpit canopy. *(M. J. Hooks.)*

Topping up a Mosquito here is a Bedford QL 1000 gallon 'Butterfield' refueller, probably on the continent later in the war. *(Percy Rodda.)*

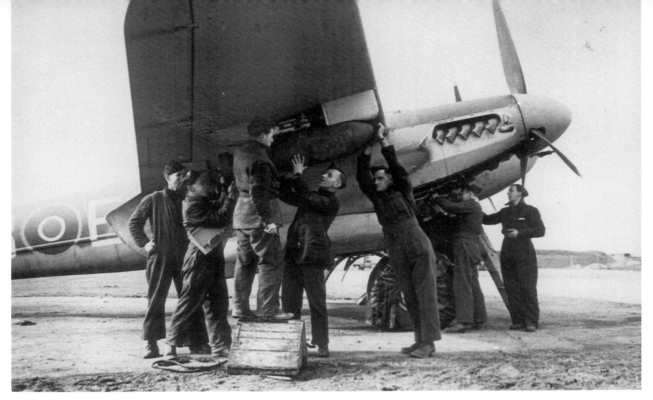

Another scene carried out thousands of times each day, that of the armourers loading up the bombs, while the ground crew carry out servicing to the starboard Merlin engine.
(Percy Rodda.)

FB.VI PZ187 arrived at Little Snoring in June 1944 to join No. 23 Squadron and was soon attacking targets over enemy-occupied Europe, and following a period in store it was sold to France. It was despatched there on 25 September, 1947.
(George Stewart.)

A standard cockpit layout for the FB.VI. At the top, directly ahead, is the blind flying panel, while below the panel are the undercarriage and flap indicators and oxygen regulators plus the levers for the bomb doors, flaps and undercarriage. To the left is the engine panel and at the top right-hand corner under the rudder trim handle are the magneto switches and the feathering buttons. The long, thin panel below this is the bomb selector panel. The instrument panels were finished in either a matt black finish or a baked-on crackle finish. In this photo only the bomb selector panel has a crackle finish, which was harder-wearing than ordinary paint. *(British Aerospace.)*

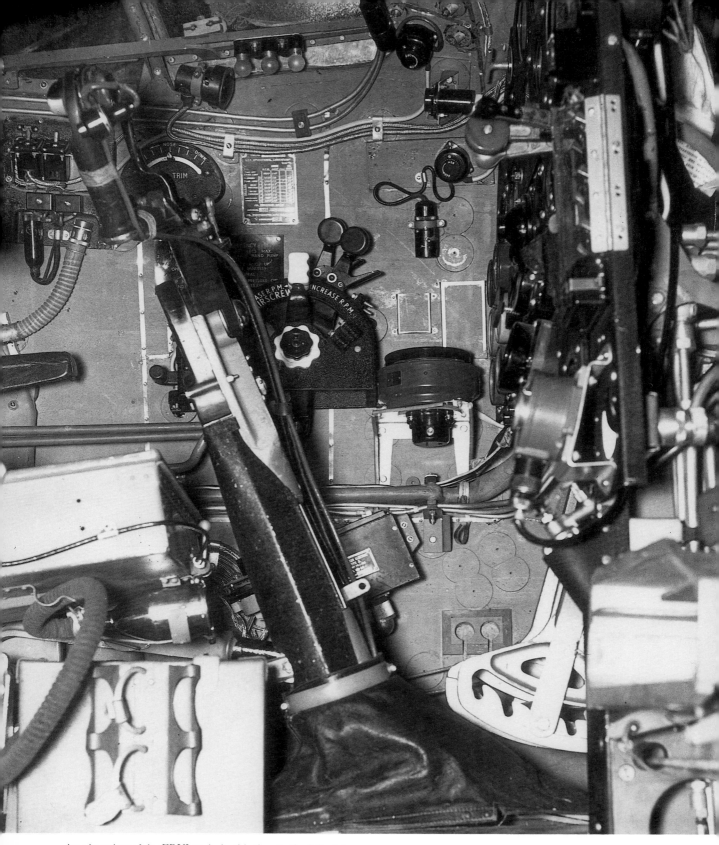

Another view of the FB.VI cockpit, this time to the left of the pilot. On the cockpit wall going upwards, right to left, is the compass, throttle quadrant, engine limitations plate, elevator trimming tab indicator and beam approach switch behind the control stick. Under the pilot's seat is the sanitary tank, first-aid locker and torch stowage. *(British Aerospace.)*

FB.VI HJ675 which left the production line at Hatfield early in
1943 was delivered to No. 301 Ferry Training Unit and then to
No. 1 Overseas Aircraft Preparation Unit at Portreath on 16
July, by which time it had been fitted out with long-range tanks,
and it left for Malta on the 21st, arriving the next day to
commence service with No. 23 Squadron at Luqa. It then
joined the squadron's other Mosquitoes on intruder operations
against targets in Sicily and along the North African coast.
HJ675 went missing on 15 January, 1944. *(RAF Museum.)*

A formation of No. 4 Squadron FB.VIs over Germany, part of
No. 140 Wing, BAFO. The squadron used their FB.VIs in
practising steep glide attacks, virtually dive bombing at some
60 degrees, as part of their routine and at least one Mosquito
shed its wings when it became over-stressed. RS678, in the
foreground, was delivered to the squadron at Gütersloh in
February 1947 and was written off on 17 June, 1948.
(via M. J. Hooks.)

The FB.XVIII was an incredible weapons platform – besides the 57 mm Molins gun, which could fire 25 six-inch shells in 23 seconds, it also carried 8 x 60 lb rockets and still retained its 4 x 303in machine guns. The machine guns helped in sighting purposes. NT225 was built at Hatfield as an FB.VI and was converted to FB.XIII standards. It was delivered to No. 248 Squadron at Banff, where it joined in the squadron's anti-shipping strikes off the Norwegian coast. It went missing on 7 December, 1944. *(MAP.)*

An FB.VI of No. 305 (Polish) Squadron at Lasham in the summer of 1944, the squadron operating almost always on night sorties into enemy occupied Europe. Precision attacks on specific targets were also a speciality. The squadron disbanded at Faldingworth on 6 January, 1947. *(J. B. Cynk.)*

FB.VIs of No. 84 Squadron at St Thomas Mount near Madras in India in January 1946. Behind the Dodge truck is the tail of a derelict Stirling of No. 46 Squadron. *(Ralph Dargue.)*

Leavesden-built T.III TV974 was despatched to the Middle East on 6 February, 1946, arriving at Khartoum, its destination, a week later. In September it returned to the UK and the following May was delivered to the Institute of Aviation Medicine at Farnborough. Four years later it was sold for scrap to Lowton Metals of Leigh near Warrington. *(MAP.)*

A closer view of the 57 mm Molins gun in the nose of a Mosquito FB.XVIII. The Molins gun was a very successful weapon, but was heavy, weighing 1580 lbs. As a fixed gun it had to be taken to and brought back from the target, and it was superseded by the rocket-carrying FB.VIs. *(via Chaz Bowyer.)*

Undergoing routine servicing are FB.VIs of Nos. 21 and 107 Squadrons at Gutersloh in 1947. Keeping an eye on the proceedings is a Humber Mk III Scout Car of the RAF Regiment. *(MAP.)*

Rather well-used T.III, RR296, of No. 8 Squadron at Layia in 1947. The code letters appear to be in a 'shadow' colour scheme, outlined in white. *(via Andy Thomas.)*

In September 1946 four T.IIIs were sold to the RNZAF by the Commonwealth Disposals Commission in Australia, as these were urgently required to convert RNZAF pilots who were to be involved in flying back to New Zealand the 80 FB.VIs that had been ordered from Britain. The four T.IIIs flew from Amberley to Norfolk Island on 7 November, 1946, flying on the next day to Whenuapai. Two of the aircraft are pictured here at Norfolk Island – A52-1006/NZ2302 and A52-1003/NZ2304. Both aircraft were sold as scrap in 1954. *(J. B. Coll.)*

Starting out as FB.40 A52-64, this Mosquito was converted to PR.41 standards and re-numbered A52-325 and served with No. 87 (Survey) Squadron and was involved in the aerial survey of Australia, which the squadron carried out from 1947 until 1953. Piloted by Flt. Sgt. Gordon with navigator Flg. Off. Mike Wood on 16 July, 1953, A52-325 completed a 2 hr 10 min flight to the Monte Bello Islands atomic explosion test site to test radiation levels on the Mosquito's unexposed film. On 29 August, A52-325 and three other Mosquitoes from No. 87 Squadron completed the last operational flight of the Mosquito in RAAF service when they flew from Port Hedland to Canberra via Alice Springs. A52-325 was flown on this flight by Sqn. Ldr. McKenzie and Sqn. Ldr. Kevin Carrick. *(via Mark Nelson.)*

FB.VI TA496 is pictured here in open storage at No. 51 MU, Lichfield, in 1947, still in the markings of No. 305 (Polish) Squadron with which it served after the war at Wahn in West Germany. Note that the wingtips have been removed. Mosquitoes that were likely to see further service were kept well maintained and sometimes flown while in store at the MUs, TA496 becoming one of 46 FB.VIs that were sold to Yugoslavia and departed from Abingdon on 7 May, 1952, re-numbered as 8092. *(John Oldacre.)*

A rather different shot of a No. 82 Squadron Mosquito FB.VI taken in the Far East. *(Vic Hewes.)*

A brand new T.III being towed out at Leavesden in the summer of 1942. After a short period in store, HJ866 left for Canada on 27 March, 1943, not arriving until the 20 April.
It was one of six T.IIIs sent by the Ministry of Aircraft Production to train Ferry Command pilots for bringing Canadian production Mosquitoes to Britain, and also for converting RCAF pilots on to the type. Note the unusual position of the serial number on the nose. *(RAF Museum.)*

FB.VI PZ471 joined No. 21 Squadron at Rosières-en-Santerre, France, in March 1945. Five months later it was damaged and did not rejoin the squadron until June 1947. No. 21 Squadron's Mosquitoes had operated a courier service from Furth to Blackbushe during the Nuremburg Trials of war criminals. PZ471 was damaged again and was returned to Leavesden for repair, but was eventually scrapped in February 1949. *(MAP.)*

A post-war shot of an FB.VI making a practice firing into the sea, having just launched four of its 60 lb rockets, the other four having been fired on an earlier run. *(Air Ministry.)*

PR.41 A52-302 (ex-FB.40 A52-193), probably taken at RAAF Fairbairn. Note the No. 87 Squadron badge and the tri-coloured spinners. While with No. 87 Squadron it went on a squadron detachment to Fiji in 1952 and New Guinea in 1953 and it was eventually sold as scrap to the R. H. Grant Trading Co in 1958. *(via Mark Nelson.)*

An armourer loads up the .303in Browning machine guns into
an FB.VI of 'B' Flight of No. 333 (Norwegian) Squadron. It was
not unknown that while unhinging the nose doors to gain
access to the machine guns an incautious right boot could
impact with and detonate the 'IFF' destructor! The 'IFF' –
Identification Friend or Foe – consisted of a transmitter which
could be triggered by a ground or airborne radar to give a coded
response which identified the source as being friendly. It was
widely used. *(via Cato Guhnfeldt.)*

Another good view of an FB.VI of 'B' Flight, No. 333 (Norwegian) Squadron, this time with the engine fitters at work on the port engine. Note that the engine side panel by the crew entry ladder, resting against the nacelle, is roughly painted 'L-STB', short for starboard, on the inside. This was a practice carried out by the ground crews on many removable panels and parts that were 'handed'. Aircraft serial numbers were also painted on panels and parts to identify which aircraft the part belongs to. *(via Cato Guhnfeldt.)*

A rather pleasing picture of FB.VI A52-504 (ex-HR335) of No. 1 Squadron, RAAF, about to touch down at Kingaroy, Queensland. No. 1 Squadron worked up on the Mosquito at Kingaroy early in 1945 and moved to Labuan Island off the coast of Borneo in July 1945 as part of No. 86 Attack Wing, RAAF, for operations against the Japanese forces in northern Borneo. The squadron officially disbanded at Narromine, NSW, on 7 August, 1946. No. 1 Squadron did in fact have to return to Australia rather sooner than expected as the fabric on the mainplanes had started to deteriorate, and without the facilities on the Labuan airstrip to re-cover the wing, the decision was made to fly the Mosquitoes home before they had to be grounded. A52-504 stayed with the squadron throughout and was put up for disposal in 1949. *(via R. A. E. Taylor.)*

Standard Motors-built RF884 was initially delivered to the aircraft pool at Bircham Newton on 15 April, 1945. It was then delivered to No. 248 Squadron a few days later at Chivenor. Moving to Thorney Island the squadron disbanded on 1 October, 1946, when it was renumbered No. 36 Squadron and operated in the coastal strike role, but was disbanded once again on 14 October, 1947. RF884 was put into store and sold as scrap to J. Coley & Sons. It is seen here at Northolt on 29 August, 1947, complete with rockets. In peacetime the machine guns were usually removed and the ports faired over; the port on the nosecone in the picture is for the camera gun. The spinners appear to be black tipped with white. *(Peter Clifton.)*

No. 4 Squadron Mosquitoes are here undergoing maintenance, probably at Wahn in 1948. 'UP-G' is undergoing a major check of its airframe and engines. In the top left-hand corner of the hangar are several spare Merlin engines. *(RAF Museum.)*

RF610 was Standard Motors-built at Coventry and was delivered to No. 248 squadron at Banff in April 1945. After a short period it was put into store and in April 1948 was allocated to the French Air Force, but instead it moved to the Armament Practice Station at Acklington in July. Back into store by October 1949 with No. 22 MU, it remained there until flown to No. 10 Ferry Unit at Abingdon as part of an order for Yugoslavia, leaving as '8114' on 10 September, 1952. In this shot, RF610 is carrying a mixed load of 100-gallon drop tanks and two 60 lb rockets under each wing. *(RAF Museum.)*

FB.XVIII PZ468 saw service with Nos. 248 and 254 Squadrons and was eventually SOC (reduced to spares) on 25 November, 1946. *(RAF Museum.)*

PZ330 arrived at Ohakea, New Zealand, on 16 July, 1947, having been delivered from the UK by Flt. Lt. E. C. Heaton and Flt. Lt. T. A. McL. Morgan. It was then allocated the number NZ2350, but was pressed into service as instructional airframe No. INST 123 at Hobsonville TTS and was eventually put up for disposal in January 1953. *(via D. A. S. MacKay and J. M. G. Gradidge.)*

'Home for Xmas' adorns the nose of FB.VI PZ196, one of the 80 aircraft ordered by New Zealand from the UK. It is pictured here *en route* at Mauripur, Karachi, on 16 November, 1947, but unfortunately PZ196, crewed by Flt. Lt. F. J. Adams and Flg. Off. M. J. Fry did not make it home for Xmas, for it crashed on take-off at Mingaladon on 26 November. The machine guns have been wrapped in fabric and then taped and the cannon ports have been faired over for the journey. The rear view mirror is not regular equipment. *(via R. C. Sturtivant.)*

Being bombed up at St Thomas Mount, Madras in India, is FB.VI RF672 of No. 45 Squadron. After preparation for tropical use at RAF Pershore it flew out to the Far East and arrived on 10 April, 1945. Peter Sorrel was a regular pilot on RF672.The squadron moved to Ceylon early in 1946 and it was probably one of several left behind because of lamination problems with the main spar.

A series of gun camera shots taken by the FB.VI of Flt. Lt. Vic Hewes of No. 82 Squadron attacking Japanese positions in Burma early in 1945. The squadron was based at Kumbhirgram.

Attacking a Japanese two-man tank on the Yamethin-Pyinmana road.

Strafing a Japanese staff car on the Iloi Kaw-He-Ho road.

Operation 21. Locomotive in Bagha on the Shweda Ya Mathin railroad.

Operation 6. Photo-recco on damaged bridge at Sinthe.

Attacking Japanese troop positions close to a Burmese village.

RF713 was built by Standard Motors and after a period in store was despatched to the Far East, where it arrived on 5 April, 1945. It is pictured here at Meiktila; note what appears to be over 50 mission symbols painted on the nose. RF713 could have been one of the Mosquitoes sent out for weathering trials. Heat and exposure soon took its toll, causing the glue to crack and the plywood skinning to lift off the spars. Some of the trials aircraft had formaldehyde glue used in their construction, and these aircraft proved to be satisfactory. Subsequently, only those Mosquitoes in which formaldehyde glue had been used were operated in the Far East.

The Operations Room at Banff of No. 333 (Norwegian) Squadron in 1944. The crews await departure of the Banff Strike Wing's attack on Sandeford Harbour on 2 April, 1945. *(via Bjorn Olsen.)*

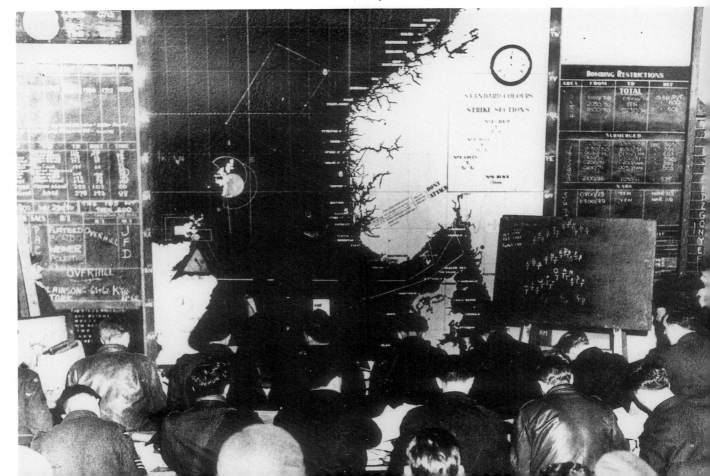

Photographic Reconnaissance

The first operational unit to operate the Mosquito was No. 1 Photographic Reconnaissance Unit at Benson in Oxfordshire, and it was there that the prototype PR Mosquito, W4051, was delivered on 13 July, 1941, followed by W4054 and W4055. It fell to W4055 to make the PR Mosquito's first operational sortie on 17 September, when Sqn. Ldr. Clerke took off to photograph Brest and the Spanish-French border. From them on Mosquitoes took over the long-range PR duties from Spitfires and its great speed made it almost immune to interception by enemy fighters. PR Mosquitoes also operated at night using American M46 photoflash equipment of 600,000 candlepower.

It was a PR Mosquito that discovered the V-weapons research centre at Peenemünde and as a result of the information that its cameras gleaned – pictures showing objects resembling rockets – Bomber Command despatched nearly 600 heavy bombers to destroy the site.

From August 1943 PR Mosquitoes operated in the Far East and missions of long duration were the rule rather than the exception; the record was claimed by a PR.34 of No. 684 Squadron, which made a nine-hour 2600-mile round trip over Penang and Taiping from the Cocos Islands on 20 August, 1945. Even after the war ended, PR Mosquitoes still played a vital role, covering the Palestine emergency and the seven-year operation to clear Communist terrorists from Malaya.

The first PR Mosquito was the PR.I, and in all ten were built and equipped with three vertical cameras and one oblique one. Next came a small number of PR.IVs, which were a straight conversion from the B.IV. The PR.VIII, a conversion based on the PR.IV but with two-stage Merlin 61s, served as a stop-gap until the PR.IX entered service, and only five were built. The PR.IX first flew in April 1943 and as well as its own internal fuel load could also carry two 200-gallon drop tanks, serving extensively at home and overseas. The PR.XVI, which first flew in July 1943, incorporated two-stage Merlins and pressure cabin and was a further development; a number of these were passed to the USAAF in England, while others were used after the war by the Royal Navy.

Based on the PR.XVI came the PR.32, which was a high-altitude version and incorporated extended wingtips and later Merlins. The ultimate PR Mosquito was the PR.34, a very long-range version specially lightened to give an increase in ceiling of 3000 ft. With extra tankage, 1269 gallons of fuel could be carried.

Australia also produced two PR versions, the PR.40, of which six were delivered to Australian squadrons, and a number of PR.41s, which were similar to the PR.IX but with Packard-built Merlins.

Banking over the Hertfordshire countryside is PR.34 RG245, clearly showing the camera ports in the bomb bay and the fuselage. The swollen bomb bay allowed for more equipment to be installed, but reduced the aircraft's speed by 6 mph TAS. RG245 was delivered to No. 540 Squadron in September 1948 and stayed until written off in May 1950. Operating out of its base at Benson, RG245 helped carry out an aerial survey of Central and West London, an area of 50 square miles, in the latter part of 1948 for a new Ordnance Survey map series of the city. It flew at 4200 ft. *(via M. J. Hooks.)*

PR.34 RG242 was delivered to Benson in June 1945, but after three months was put into store. After flying to Marshalls at Cambridge in January 1947 for modifications, it was again put into storage until it departed for the Middle East on 9 November, 1949, where it joined No. 13 Squadron at Fayid in Egypt. Here it helped in the aerial survey of most of the Mediterranean countries until arriving back in the UK in March 1952 after the squadron's Mosquitoes were replaced by Meteors. It was then sold to D. Bland on 31 May, 1954. Note the silver top surface, which was applied as a protection against the sun. *(via Jim D. Oughton.)*

PR.34a RG314 was delivered to No. 540 Squadron at Benson in December 1945. In 1950 it spent some time at de Havilland to overcome rogue characteristics and was later delivered to No. 81 Squadron at Tengah. Here it helped plot terrorist movements over the jungles of Malaya, a 12-year long campaign known as Operation 'Firedog'. It fell to No. 81 Squadron and RG314 to fly the last operational Mosquito flight in the RAF on 15 December, 1955, crewed by Flg. Off. 'Collie' Knox and Flg. Off. 'Tommy' Thompson. It is seen here making a low fly-past for the benefit of the cameras at Seletar, Singapore. Note also the remains of a Mosquito on the airfield dump just below the tail of RG314.

Taken on strength by the RAF at Benson on 10 November, 1943, PR.IX LR480 was a month later prepared for overseas duty and flown to the Middle East, where it joined No. 60 Squadron, South African Air Force. It is seen here at San Severo in Italy, from where it flew many sorties over the Balkans and Austria. On 14 December, 1944, Col. Glynn Davies, a former CO of No. 60 Squadron, flew an attempted record-breaking flight in LR480 from Cairo to Pretoria with Brig. Hingeston as observer, but the aircraft was damaged landing at Que-Que in Rhodesia. It was later repaired and flown to South Africa, where it now resides in the South African National Museum of Military History at Saxonwold, Johannesburg. *(via Ken Smy.)*

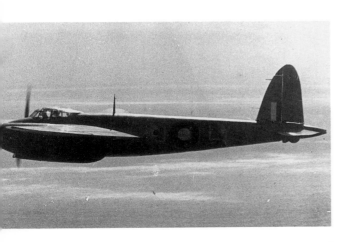

Silhouetted against the sun here is the veteran Salisbury Hall-built PR.I prototype W4051. After assembly at Hatfield it made its first flight on 10 June, 1941 and, only a month later, on 13 July, it arrived at No. 1 Photographic Reconnaissance Unit at Benson to start its operational career. Some of its sorties included a trip to Kiel, where it photographed the *Geneisnau* in dry dock, and in March 1942 photographed the French coast prior to the Commando raid on St. Nazaire. On 20 September it joined No. 521 Squadron at Bircham Newton, but not for long, as ten days later it flew to Benson for service with No. 540 Squadron. Its operational days over it was passed to No 8 OTU at Dyce in August 1943 and crashed on 19 July, 1944. It was transported to Hatfield for repair, but was instead written off on 22 June, 1945. *(via Jim D. Oughton.)*

PR.34 VL618 was delivered straight into storage from Hatfield, where it remained until June 1947, when it was delivered to the Fighter Command Communication Squadron. In April 1950 it was again stored until despatched to No. 13 Squadron in Egypt in November, where it was involved in a flying accident and was SOC on 13 March, 1951. In operational service the long-range PR.34s career in the Far East started in June 1945, when the first examples joined a detachment of No. 684 Squadron on the Cocos Islands. *(Flight International.)*

Based on the prototype, W4050, ten PR.Is were built, four of which were long-range aircraft and two which were tropicalized. They were equipped with three vertical cameras and one oblique and all PR.Is had short nacelles, as can be seen here on W4059 at Benson, where it flew operationally with No. 1 PRU. *(MAP.)*

The PR XVI RG116, seen here, was fitted with two-stage
Merlins and also incorporated a pressure cabin, first flying in
July 1943. Delivered to Benson in January 1945, RG116 was
shortly afterwards allocated to No. 34 Wing in April, but just
five months later was put into store, from where it was sold as
scrap to BRL Alloys on 28 April, 1948. *(J. M. Bruce/S. Leslie
Collection.)*

Like many PR.34s RG248 started its career at Benson, where it was delivered in June 1945, but in December 1946 it joined the Meteorological Research Flight at the RAE, Farnborough. In early 1954 it was put into storage and was allocated for spares breakdown by No. 34 MU on 16 October, 1954. The top surface of the aircraft appears to be painted white; note also the curious modification set into the fuselage just in front of the roundel. *(MAP.)*

Constructed at Hatfield in June 1946, RG236 went straight into storage with No. 27 MU at Shawbury and did not emerge until February 1949, when it was loaned for three months to Marshalls' Flying School for modifications. It then joined No. 540 Squadron at Benson for nearly two years until it was delivered across the airfield to No. 237 OCU and finally to No. 231 OCU at Bassingbourn two months later. Note the No. 540 Squadron badge on the fin. *(RAF Museum.)*

PR. 34 RG300 was delivered to the Photographic Reconnaissance Development Unit at Benson in September 1946, passing in turn to Nos. 58 and 540 Squadrons on the same airfield. In September 1946 there was an Aeronautical Exhibition in Buenos Aires and RG300 was selected to attend as a goodwill gesture. Flown by Wg. Cdr. S. McCreith with Flt. Lt. Freddie Thayer as navigator, RG300 took off from Benson on 22 September and after a quick turn-around at Gibraltar they headed for the West African coast, but could not make radio contact. They decided to divert into RAF Yundum at Bathurst using their radio beacon for a homing, but while waiting at the end of the runway for taxi instructions the starboard wingtip was rammed by a fire tender. RG300 had to be left behind and VL613 was flown out as a replacement, arriving at Buenos Aires on 3 October. RG300 was flown home and was eventually sold to Jack Amman Photogrammetric Engineers in San Antonio, Texas, on 31 October, 1956, one of five Mosquitoes bought by Amman from the Air Ministry. RG300 became N9871F and carried out contract survey work in the USA until 1959, when, together with N9868F (PF670) it was parked at San Antonio and left. The remains of RG300 were subsequently rescued by the Confederate Air Force, who eventually passed them to Jim Merizan for possible use in his restoration project.
(via S. McCreith).

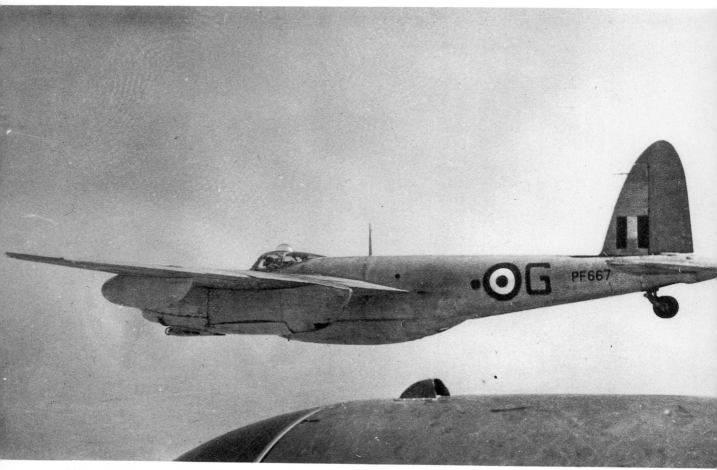

Although laid down as a B.XVI, Percival-built PF667 was modified on the production line to PR.34 standards, emerging from the Luton factory early in 1946. It could carry a fuel load of 1269 gallons, including the two 200-gallon drop tanks, and a further 1192 gallons could be carried in a fuselage belly tank. PF667 spent its operational time with No. 13 Squadron at Fayid in Egypt and after suffering damage was SOC in January 1950. *(via Dave Welch.)*

After the war there were many surplus Mosquitoes. Most were stored in the open and soon became unfit to fly. Here at Cherhill are two derelict PR.34s in poor condition in 1958, with the engines of RG267 already gone, perhaps to keep a flying example in the air. After the removal of the remaining metal content, the airframe would be burnt. *(MAP.)*

The PR.IV was a day and night photographic-reconnaissance conversion of the B.IV Series ii and first flew in April 1942. DZ383 saw service with No. 540 Squadron at Benson and was finally scrapped on 31 October, 1946.

Twenty-three PR.XVIs were imported into Australia, most of which saw service with No. 87 Squadron RAAF in the Far East and Australia. A52-610 (ex-NS727) is seen here at Coomalie Creek in northern Australia in August 1945. It was sold in 1955 to Wilmore Aviation as scrap. *(Frank F. Smith.)*

A PR.40, A52-6 of No. 87 Squadron, RAAF, seen at Coomalie Creek in December 1944. Six PR.40s, which were similar to the PR.IX, were built by de Havilland at their Bankstown factory and then the PR.40 was replaced by the PR.41 on the production line. *(Frank F. Smith.)*

A lovely view of PR.XVI NS705 on a pre-delivery flight from Hatfield in September 1944. After delivery to Benson it left for the Mediterranean, where it went missing on 20 January, 1945. *(Charles E. Brown/RAF Museum.)*

In 1954 Spartan Air Services of Ottawa purchased 15 Mosquito B.35s (including one PR.35) from the Air Ministry for use in their survey operations in Canada. Ten were overhauled by Derby Aviation Ltd at Burnaston near Derby and were ferried to Canada. The remaining five were ferried to Hurn. Three, CF-IMA, 'IMC and 'IMD were dismantled and shipped to Canada as a source of spares, while 'IMB and 'IME were stripped of useful spares and just left. Only a few years ago the author came across two wing sections in the by then well overgrown area in which they had been left. Note in this photograph the crude application of the Canadian civil markings applied even to the aircraft that were used for spares. *(Roy Bonser.)*

Seen here at Burnaston in 1955 is one of the ten airworthy Spartan B.35s, CF-HMP, ex-TK648. After overhaul by Derby Aviation Ltd., it was ferried to Ottawa by Peter Nock. It departed from Derby on 22 September, 1955 via Prestwick and reached Keflavik, Iceland on 25 September. On the next leg of the flight engine failure necessitated a return to Keflavik and after an engine change it departed on 27 October via Sondrestrom and Goose Bay to Ottawa where it arrived two days later. After modifications it carried out its survey tasks, including a job in South America early in 1956 when it was flown by Al McNutt as a replacement aircraft for CF-HMN (TA713) which he had to put down in a field near Bogota in Colombia and was written off. On 10 September, 1957 'HMP was crashed and burnt out 16 miles NNE of Neepawa, Manitoba on a ferry flight from Edmonton to Winnipeg. *(M.J. Hooks)*

These four views illustrate the activities of No. 627 Squadron at Woodhall Spa in 1944 and are 'stills' taken from unique colour footage shot by Brian Harris, a navigator on the squadron. Shown are B.IVs and a B.XX. *(Brian Harris)*

The first-ever crossing of the Atlantic by jet fighters was made by six Vampires of No. 54 Squadron. Escorted by three Mosquitoes of No. 1 Ferry Unit, together with three Avro Yorks carrying spares and ground crews, they left Odiham on 1 July, 1948. The Vampires were hampered by strong winds and the group did not reach Goose Bay until the 15th. The Mosquitoes, PR.34s PF620, PF621 and PF623 did the navigation and scouted ahead of the group reporting the weather conditions back to their charges. The Vampires performed a number of displays in Canada and when they travelled south into the USA they were escorted by PF620, seen here at Andrews Air Force Base, Washington, on 25 July piloted by Sqdn. Ldr. H.B. ('Mickey') Martin and Navigator 2 Simpson. The group left Goose Bay on 17 August, arriving Stornaway on the 25th after a very successful tour. *(via Dave Ostrowski)*

T.III, RR299, landing at the Farnborough Air Show in September 1966 to take part in the display. It was piloted by Pat Fillingham who was a production test pilot at Hatfield during the war. After service with No. 3 CAACU, RR299 was acquired by Hawker Siddeley Aviation on 10 July, 1963. *(Roy Bonser.)*

B.35, RS709, seen here while it was residing with the Confederate Air Force at Harlingen, Texas before returning to the UK in November 1979. It was photographed in October 1973 and is now back in the USA with the USAF Museum at Dayton, Ohio, where it has been converted to represent a PR.XVI of the USAAF, Circa 1944-5. *(Stuart Howe.)*

Mosquito B.35, CF-HML, near completion after a long and thorough rebuild. Formerly VR796, it is an ex-Spartan Airways aircraft, and after it was withdrawn from use it was bought by Don Campbell and transported to Kapuskasing in Ontario where restoration to flying condition was commenced by the Air Cadets. In 1979 arrangements were made to have the Mosquito's restoration finished at Mission, British Columbia. This photograph was taken on 12 May, 1984, since when there has been very little progress on the aircraft, partly because of a lack of funds, and the aircraft is now in the safe keeping of the Canadian Museum of Flight and Transportation.
(Jerry B. Vernon)

On 15 August, 1944, Captain Pienaar and Lt. Archie Lockhart-Ross of No. 60 Squadron, SAAF, took off from San Severo in PR.XVI NS520 to photograph Gunzburg and Leipheim, and while in the target area they were intercepted by an Me 262 jet fighter. The jet attacked 12 times over a period of 40 minutes, but Pienaar out manoevred the Me 262 each time. When NS520 made a wheels-up landing back in Italy it was seen to have lost in the attacks its entire port flaps and the rear of the nacelle, as well as its tailcone and some of the port tailplane. Both Capt. Pienaar and Lt. Archie Lockhart-Ross were immediately awarded the DFC. *(British Aerospace.)*

A shot of PR.34 RG264 of No. 81 Squadron in 1951, on a sortie over the Malayan countryside. *(MAP.)*

PR.XVI MM335 found itself Mediterranean-bound in March 1944 to join No. 680 Squadron at Matariya, where it is pictured, and then San Severo, where it joined in the squadron's activities over the Balkans. In February 1946 the squadron moved to Aqir in Egypt, where it undertook survey flights over neighbouring territories, with a final move to Ein Shemer in Palestine, and it was here that MM335 was SOC.

A pre-delivery photograph of PR.IX MM230. It was used for a while by de Havilland for exhaust shroud tests and was also used by the Fighter Interception Unit at Ford as a target aircraft.

PR.41 A52-300 started out as FB.40 A52-90, the conversion entailing the fitting of Merlin 69s, extra radio gear, long-range oil tanks, extra oxygen and enlarged radiators. A52-300 served with No. 1 APU and was sold as scrap to the R. H. Grant Trading Co. in 1958.

Even at this angle and despite the swollen bomb-bay and
200-gallon drop tanks, the beautiful lines of the Mosquito are
still apparent. The subject this time is VL619, a PR.34 which
served with No. 13 Squadron at Fayid and was SOC in
September 1951. *(RAF Museum.)*

A pair of PR.34s flying along the Suez Canal. These were used in the Middle East for several years after the war and were used to cover the Palestine emergency. A range in excess of 2500 miles could be attained by this version.

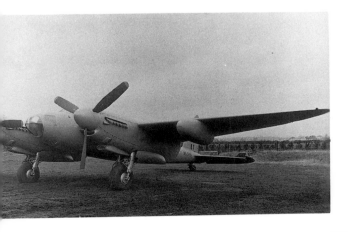

A factory-taken shot of PR.32 NS589 at Hatfield in October 1944, before it was flown to Benson to join No. 540 Squadron. It became the first PR.32 to see operational service when Wg. Cdr. H. W. Ball and Flt. Lt. Leatham took off on 5 December, 1944, to photograph Darmstadt and Mannheim, during which they were intercepted by two enemy fighters. During its 14 operations, NS589 was used exclusively to photograph the German railway network. The PR.32 was based on the PR.XVI, but was specially lightened for high-altitude work and had extended wingtips, giving a span of 59 ft 2 in. It first flew in August 1944. *(British Aerospace.)*

The following are examples of the sort of work the photographic reconnaissance Mosquitoes carried out (these target photographs are courtesy Mrs Ethel Gurney via Martin Taylor. NB. Mrs Gurney's husband, Maj. C. S. C. Gurney, produced de Havilland's now classic private venture film *Mosquito* shortly after the war):

Königsberg burning after the first RAF bomber attack.

Peenemünde Experimental Station after an RAF heavy bomber
attack in August 1943. Over 50 aircraft are visible, including
transport and bomber types on the right.

Toulon – the scuttled French fleet on 27 November, 1942.

Tripoli harbour with the booms open to allow a ship to enter.
There are also several twin-engined flying boats at anchor.

The important airfield and factory of Wiener-Neustadt near
Vienna, which built the Messeischmitt Bf109, a number of
which can be seen lined up on the airfield.

RG176 was the first PR.34 built but after construction was
sent to Marshalls for conversion to PR.34a in May, 1950, after
which it was delivered to 540 Sq at Benson in July, 1951 but
less than a year later it was damaged and reduced to spares by
58 MU in June 1952.

Sea Mosquito

In 1943 the Admiralty considered the use of the Mosquito as a carrier-borne aircraft, but was not sure if a large twin-engined aircraft like the Mosquito could operate successfully from a carrier deck. The outcome was that FB.VI LR359 was allocated for carrier trials and was modified by de Havilland by the introduction of an arrester hook mounted under the rear fuselage. In order to withstand the high loadings that occur during arrested landings, the rear fuselage was reinforced with additional longerons and for the trials the armament was removed in order to save weight. Wing folding was not introduced until later.

LR359 was delivered to Farnborough in January 1944 to prepare it for carrier trials and on the 25th commenced take-offs and landings on a dummy deck marked out on the runway. A second FB.VI, LR387, joined LR359 and both were flown up to RNAS Arbroath on 18 March, where LR387 was used for arrester gear trials using arrester wires installed across the runway. Further trials were carried out at East Haven, and on the satisfactory conclusion of these trials both aircraft were flown to Machrihanish on 23 March. On the 25th Lt. E. M. Brown made a successful landing on HMS *Indefatigable* using LR359, making history as the first ever deck landing by a twin-engined aircraft.

In November, LR387 was returned to Hatfield to become fully navalized as the prototype TR.33. Modifications included the introduction of manually folding outer wings, American ASH radar, four-bladed propellers, RATOG gear and oleo-pneumatic landing gear, which replaced the rubber-in-compression legs in the naval version. The armament consisted of four 20mm cannon and provision for an under-belly 2000lb torpedo or bomb or mine. The normal under-wing loads of the FB.VI could also be carried. Fifty production TR.33s were built, although only one frontline unit, No. 811 Squadron, operated it. Several second-line squadrons used the TR.33 until June 1953.

The next naval variant was the TF.37 with ASV Mk XIII radar, but otherwise similar to the TR.33. This was followed by the TT.39 which was a target-tug conversion based on the B.XVI. The design and conversion work was carried out by General Aircraft Ltd at Hanworth. This provided for a camera operator in the extended and glazed nose and an observer in a dorsal cupola located just aft of the wing's trailing edge. The length of the fuselage was increased to 43ft 4in overall and 24 production TT.39s were built, serving at home and from Hal Far, Malta, until phased out of service in May 1952. The Royal Navy also operated a number of ex-RAF Mosquitoes, the majority of which were the FB.VI, PR.XVI and T.III versions.

FB.VI TE711 of No. 811 Squadron during a practice formation flight on 20 May, 1946, in preparation for the victory flypast over London on 8 June, 1946. No. 811 Squadron was re-formed at Ford on 15 September, 1945, equipped with 15 FB.VIs and in 1946 it received the TR.33. *(via Bill Holdrick.)*

Another view of No. 811 Squadron's Mosquitoes in close
formation practising for the 1946 victory flypast over London.
The Squadron was one of four FAA squadrons that took part in
this event. In the foreground is TE720, flown by Lt. J.
Culbertson with Bill Holdrick as his observer. John Culbertson
carried out the deck landing trials aboard HMS *Illustrious* in the
TR.33 in October 1946. TE720 was transferred directly to the
Royal Navy on 27 August, 1945, and after No. 811 Squadron it
went on to serve with Nos. 790, 703 and 751 Squadrons and
early in 1953 it was placed into storage at Lossiemouth, from
where it was sold to R. A. Short in November, and after
overhaul at Blackbushe was then delivered to Israel. Parts of
TE720 still exist today, for when the Mosquito Aircraft
Museum recovered the wing of TR.33 TW233 from Israel in
1980 it contained parts from TE720 as well as other parts from
TR449, one of the prototype TR.33s. *(via Bill Holdrick.)*

The Navy also had quite a number of PR.XVIs, which were used for training and Fleet Requirements duties. Many of these were also later bought for the Israeli Air Force. *(via Bill Holdrick.)*

TR.33 TW292 of No. 771 Squadron taken in 1947. No. 771 Squadron was a Fleet Requirements Unit (FRU) based at Lee-on-Solent with a number of different aircraft types, but as the runways at Lee were not suitable for the Mosquito, these were based at Ford, mainly on radar trials. 'LP' on the fin was the code for Lee-on-Solent. *(via Bill Holdrick)*

Sea Mosquito TR.33 TW286 of No. 771 Squadron photographed at RNAS Ford in 1947. The TR.33 was fitted with AI Mk XV (US designation AN/APS4), but in fact this equipment was not an Airborne Interception radar but as Air-to-Surface radar, more commonly known as ASH. It could be used at fairly low level and had a range of 3.75 miles and its relatively slow scan speed meant that it could also be used as a navigational aid. Sometimes firing the guns produced sufficient vibration to render the radar unserviceable! *(via Bill Holdrick.)*

About to touch down at Ford is FB.VI TE823 of No. 762
Squadron, which was a Heavy Twin Conversion Unit used for
training the Navy's Mosquito pilots. The squadron also had
T.IIIs. The squadron was disbanded at Culdrose on 8
December, 1949. TE823 swung on take-off at Ford on 10
April, 1946, and the starboard undercarriage collapsed. It was
probably written off. *(Bill Holdrick.)*

This rather unfortunate F.II, DZ761, smashes down on the deck of an aircraft carrier, breaking off its starboard wing, nose and tail section, but on closer inspection the engines have not been turning, and note the rig attached to the tail. Judging by the height of the rig the Mosquito must have been very tail high. DZ761 was transferred to the Royal Navy on research and development work in December 1946, after the deck landing trials by manned Mosquitoes, so just what sort of experiment was being undertaken here? DZ761 started out with No. 264 Squadron at Predannack in April 1943, then with Nos. 307 and 141 Squadrons and finally with No. 1692 Bomber Support Training Flight at Gt. Massingham. Here it suffered Category 'B' damage in September 1944 and was delivered to Martin Hearn for repair, but was recategorized 'E' (written off), most likely to enable it to be used for the experiment shown. It was initially delivered to RNAS Gosport after transfer to the Royal Navy. *(Peter Cook.)*

The wings of the Sea Mosquito had to be folded manually, as seen on this series of photos of the prototype TR.33 LR387 on 12 June, 1945, at Hatfield. In the first shot the hinge of the wing fold can clearly be seen and the support strut for the folded wing, which appears to be hydraulic. The TR.33 had four-bladed propellers and oleo-pneumatic landing gear in place of the normal rubber-in-compression. As seen here an 18in Mk XV or XVII torpedo could be carried as well as the normal underwing loads of an FB.VI. Another option was RATOG (Rocket Assisted Take-Off Gear), which consisted of two detachable RATO bottles on each side of the lower fuselage that dropped away after being fired. *(British Aerospace via Jim D. Oughton.)*

The TT.39 was produced exclusively for the Royal Navy and surely has to take the prize of being the ugliest Mosquito variant produced. Based on the B.XVI airframe, some 26 aircraft were modified by General Aircraft Limited at Feltham, Middlesex, to fit the Navy's target towing requirements. This called for two further crew positions, the camera operator in the new extended glass nose and the observer and drogue operator's position in a dorsal cupola aft of the wings. The new nose increased the fuselage length to 43ft 4in, and because of the width of the new nose the propeller blades had to be cropped. The TT.39 was also used for radar calibration work. PF606 does not appear to have entered squadron service, but spent some time at the RAE, Farnborough, and on radio trials at Boscombe Down and was eventually SOC at Lossiemouth on 27 November, 1952. *(RAF Museum.)*

Another fine view of No. 811 Squadron Mosquitoes practising for the 1946 victory flypast over London. *(via Bill Holdrick.)*

FB.VI LR359 was modified into the prototype Sea Mosquito with a reinforced fuselage, arrester hook and four-bladed propellers for increased power, but with the normal fixed wing. Seen here about to touch down, LR359 carried out deck landing trials on HMS *Indefatigable* off the Scottish coast on 25 and 26 March, 1944, flown by Lt. Cdr. E. M. Brown, and in so doing became the first twin-engined aircraft to land on the deck of an aircraft carrier. The Mosquito had to land to one side of the deck's centre-line to avoid hitting the island.

Another view of LR359, this time taking off and clearing the deck quite comfortably. *(Royal Aircraft Establishment via Jim D. Oughton.)*

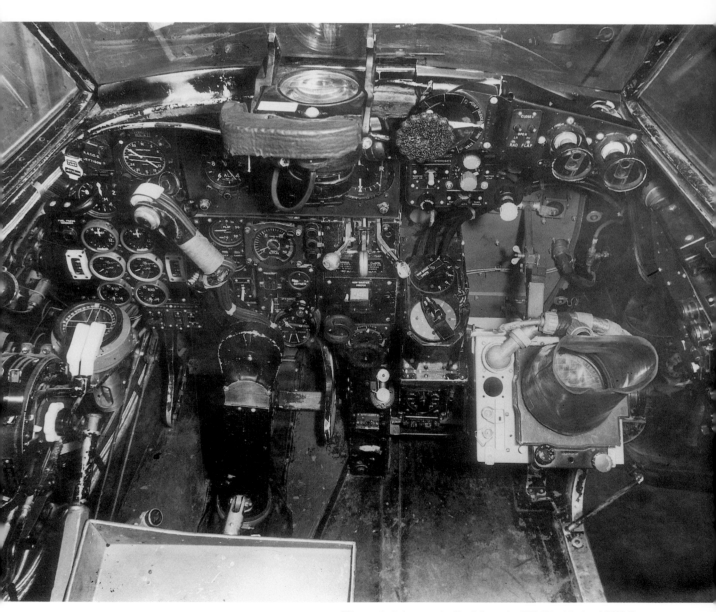

The cockpit layout of a Sea Mosquito TF.37 with the ASV Mk XIII indicator unit at the lower right. The TF.37 was similar to the TR.33 and first flew in 1946. *(British Aerospace.)*

MOSQUITO MK. (PROTOTYPE)

LR387 was the second prototype TR.33 and incorporated the upward folding wing, although at this stage the Lockeed oleo pneumatic undercarriage legs had still to be fitted. (RAF Museum.)

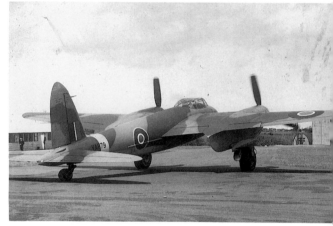

A brand new T.III, VA879, just delivered in 1947 to HMS *Vulture* shore base at St. Merryn in Cornwall, which housed the School of Naval Air Warfare. *(Ron Farley via F. H. Bradbeer and E. A. Pitcher.)*

T.III VT626 joined the Royal Navy when it was delivered to No. 2 Aircraft Receipt and Despatch Unit at Culham on 21 February, 1949, and then went into store until, in December 1953, it was flown to the civilian-operated Airwork FRU at St. Davids near Pembroke for training purposes. It was SOC on 11 September, 1958. The letters 'BY' on the fin was the code for RNAS Brawdy, St. Davids being a relief airfield for this base. (Colin Bruce.)

The popularity of the 'Micky Mouse' cartoon character was such that it appeared on many aircraft and the Mosquito was no exception, as seen here painted on the nose of a TR.33 of No. 811 Squadron, Ford. *(David Hughes.)*

TR.33 TW256 taken while it was serving with No. 771
Squadron at Lee-on-Solent late in 1948. By January 1950 it was
with the Airwork FRU at St. Davids and then Hurn until April
1953, when an engine failed on take-off and the undercarriage
collapsed as the aircraft reached the end of the runway. After
removal to Lossiemouth it was SOC two months later.
(Charles E. Brown/RAF Museum.)

Undergoing engine maintenance at Lee-on-Solent is TR.33
TW280 of No. 771 Squadron in 1948, having previously served
with No. 739 Squadron at Culham. In October 1952 it was put
into storage at Stretton and a year later it embarked on a new
career when it was sold to R. A. Short for delivery to Israel.
(MAP.)

A starboard undercarriage collapse on VA880, a T.III of No.
762 Squadron at Culdrose on 31 October, 1946. *(FAA Museum.)*

An optional fit was RATOG (Rocket Assisted Take-Off Gear)
and seen here are the two detachable RATO bottles on the port
side. *(British Aerospace.)*

Foreign Air Forces

With foreign air forces struggling to re-form after the war, the Mosquito became the ideal choice for many of them, as it was readily available and the majority of aircraft had very little time on their airframes. Nearly 1000 Mosquitoes saw service with overseas air forces.

The Royal Canadian Air Force kept part of its own production for use in Canada, as did the Royal Australian Air Force, which kept its own production as well as 75 FB.VIs and PR.XVIs received from the UK. The Royal New Zealand Air Force received 76 FB.VIs plus a few T.IIIs, T.43s and an FB.40. The versatile FB.VI was bought in far greater numbers than any other mark of Mosquito.

In April 1944 B.IV DK296 was handed over to the Soviet Union, and No. 333 (Norwegian) Squadron took its FB.VIs back to Norway and obtained further examples to supplement these. Another big post-war user was France, which bought over 100 Mosquitoes, mainly FB.VIs, but also the PR.XVI and NF.30, and Belgium purchased two FB.VIs and 24 NF.30s.

Elsewhere, Turkey received 96 FB.VIs and 10 T.IIIs, while Yugoslavia operated 46 FB.VIs, 60 NF.38s and a few T.IIIs. Czechoslovakia also acquired some FB.VIs

and Sweden 60 NF.XIXs, while for a short time the South African Air Force operated some PR.XVIs, PR.IXs and F.IIs.

Israel also acquired a considerable number of Mosquitoes from the UK and France, but due to the way in which some of these were obtained the exact figure may never be known for certain. In 1947 the Canadian Government sold over 200 Mosquitoes to the Chinese Nationalist Government; during the war some Canadian production was transferred south to the USA, and in Europe the USAAF received a number of PR.XVIs and NF.30s. In South America the Dominican Republic operated a small number of FB.VIs.

Sales of these Mosquitoes from the UK were handled in some cases directly by the Government, while others were sold by the manufacturer or private arms dealers. The aircraft were prepared for their new owners by the RAF or private overhaul facilities such as Fairey Aviation at Ringway. They were then ferried out by military or civilian crews, and it says something for the reliability of the Mosquito that very few were lost *en route*, despite the great distances covered.

The Turkish Air Force took delivery of 60 FB.VIs and ten T.IIIs shortly after the war; this photograph shows a Standard Motors-built FB.VI, but very little has come to light about Turkish use of the Mosquito. *(MAP.)*

An all-white T.III on pre-delivery flight out of Hatfield with Pat Fillingham at the controls. Some of the T.IIIs in Turkey carried 500 lb bombs beneath the wings. *(British Aerospace.)*

The Chinese Nationalist Government had long been interested in the Mosquito and during the latter half of 1947 made a deal with the Canadian government to purchase a number of Mosquitoes, reported to be worth $10 – $12 million. Rather than risk the long over-water flights it was decided to dismantle the Mosquitoes for transport by ship to Shanghai, and then reassemble the aircraft at the military airfield of Tazang, 40 miles north of Shanghai. The reassembly was to be carried out under de Havilland supervision and the test flying carried out by DH pilots. Some 205 Mosquitoes are thought to have been shipped to China, the majority of which were FB.26s, but also T.29s with a few T.27s, one T.22 and one B.25. Here we have two FB.26s on test near Shanghai. The camera aircraft was flown by George Stewart, who was one of several Canadian pilots employed by the Chinese Nationalists as a flying instructor on the Mosquito. *(George Stewart.)*

The CAF wanted three operational Mosquito units, Nos.1, 3 and 4 Sauadrons, which were operating the B.25 at the time. The first Mosquitoes arrived in February 1948, and after test flights were flown to Hankow, where the CAF pilots were to be trained. Hankow was on the Yangtse River, 400 miles inland from Shanghai, and was home to several other CAF units. The insignia of No. 3 Squadron is pictured here on the nose of an FB.26 at Hankow. *(George Stewart.)*

An FB.26 undergoing maintenance at Hankow. The CAF pilots did not quite have the physical strength of their Western counterparts and their small size also caused some difficulty in controlling the aircraft, but it was very poor maintenance by CAF personnel that was the major problem. Some 50 aircraft were lost in training. Before Tazang had to be abandoned before the advancing Communists, about 181 Mosquitoes had been assembled, of which 144 had been test flown by 4 December, 1948. *(George Stewart.)*

The CAF found the Mosquito to be more than satisfactory in combat, but the Nationalists were on the retreat and all of the remaining airworthy Mosquitoes were flown to Formosa. The Canadian contingent left for home on 17 December 1948, taking with them great admiration for the Chinese pilots, who, despite in many cases their lack of good English, mastered the Mosquito. Here T.29 'T-85' (ex-KA155) is being refuelled at Hankow. The 'T' stood for Trainer and the 85 was a shortened version of its CAF serial number B-M085, the 'M' also standing for Mosquito. The Chinese Air Force Museum at Datongshon, to the north of Peking, today houses a Mosquito. It is mainly a replica, as only part of the wing is original. *(George Stewart.)*

The Czech Air Force received at least 19 FB.VIs and was known in the Czech designation system as the B-36. Because of a lack of suitable ammunition, some of the Mosquito's armament was replaced by weapons of German origin, although in this photograph of the Mosquitoes of the Atlantic Squadron at Pilzen, the machine guns appear to have been taken out. *(Stan Spurny.)*

RF838 started its career with No. 404 Squadron, RCAF, at Banff in March 1945, and when the squadron disbanded two months later it went to No. 132 OCU at East Fortune. In February 1946 it went into store until sold to Czechoslovakia on 5 June, 1947. *(Stan Spurny.)*

This Czech Air Force Mosquito has just made a successful belly landing, but the prop-shaft on the port engine has broken off because of the impact; the unbent state of the propellers indicates that they must have been under little or no power for the landing. *(Milan Janac.)*

FL/1 Mansfield is here performing for the benefit of Yugoslavian officers over three C-3s (Siebel 204D) on a Czech Air Force base with the Mosquito's port engine feathered. The Mosquito's service in Czechoslovakia came to an abrupt end – during a flying display the Mosquitoes were among a number of aircraft types put through their paces in front of a number of high-ranking Russian officers and officials, and when the Russians enquired as to where the Mosquito had been manufactured, and was told England, they immediately ordered that the Mosquitoes be destroyed. No sooner had the engines stopped after the display than the Mosquitoes were hauled off and burnt. Only an engine remains today, at the Czech Air Force Museum at Kbely near Prague. *(Stan Spurny.)*

B.IV DK296 flew at least 15 operational missions, including the first sortie carried out by No. 139 Squadron, with whom it carried out two sorties, after which it joined No. 105 Squadron at Marham on 21 June, 1942. While with the squadron it suffered a bird strike on one sortie and on another collected a chimney pot! DK296 was also the lead aircraft on the famous low-level assault on the Gestapo headquarters in Oslo on 25 September, 1942, when it was flown by Sqn. Ldr. D. A. G. Parry, DSO, DFC. In August 1943 it went to No. 10 MU, where it was allocated to Russia, and is seen here at Errol awaiting its delivery flight in September. It finally left for Russia on 25 March, 1944, and was presumed to have arrived by 31 August. Nothing further is known about this aircraft after its arrival. *(British Aerospace.)*

Another view of DK296 at Errol. Although still retaining its serial number, the roundel and fin flash have been painted out and replaced by the red star. *(British Aerospace.)*

In the spring of 1948 the Swedish Government ordered 60 refurbished NF.XIXs to form the nucleus of Sweden's first modern air defence. These Mosquitoes also incorporated a number of modifications, including four-bladed propellers. Deliveries began in July 1948 from Hatfield to Västerås or Bromma in Sweden, where the Mosquito was known as the J30. All aircraft were allocated to the F1 Wing at Västerås and distributed to three squadrons; 1st (red), 2nd (blue) and 3rd (yellow). This aircraft, serial 30003, is seen on its delivery flight and still carries its RAF serial number, TA281, Coded red 'C', it crashed not long after in May 1949. *(via Peter Kempe.)*

30001 (TA286), the first Mosquito to be delivered at Västerås in July 1948, painted for its delivery flight in silver overall with black spinners, with the call-sign 'I' above the serial. Later to become red 'A', it served until August 1952. Note the Saab B181B in the background. *(via Peter Kempe.)*

30021 at F1 Västerås in March 1949. Blue 'B' was the last J30 to fly with the RSwAF (March 1955), some six months after the type had been withdrawn from service. The Mosquitoes were withdrawn earlier than planned due to a number of crashes, caused by both poor weather conditions and also structural failures. Under certain unfavourable flying conditions the elevator counterbalance lever broke, causing the elevator to fully extend and exposing the aircraft to such a strain that it broke up. The levers were then modified. Despite this the Mosquitoes were withdrawn and replaced by the Venom.

J30 (30031) red 'N' at Västerås. The 'N' was repeated on the nose. *(via Peter Kempe.)*

26 NF.30s were ordered by Belgium from RAF surplus stocks, under the 'Western Defence Pact', of which two were used for ground instruction and another crashed in England on 11 June, 1953, but the latter example (RK935) was flown to Belgium in two C-119s and was then written off with a total flight time of 3 hours. The 24 airworthy NF.30s were designated MB-1 to 24 and after overhaul by Fairey Aviation at Ringway, Manchester, deliveries commenced in November 1947. Servicing in Belgium was undertaken by Fairey at Gosselies. MB-20 started its RAF career as NT330 in December 1944 and served with Nos. 85 and 239 Squadrons, and during this time it destroyed a Bf 110 over Goch on the night of 7/8 February, 1945, and a Ju 188 over Nuremberg on 17/18 March. NT330 was delivered to the BAF as MB-20 on 21 December, 1948, for service with No. 10 Squadron, No. 1 Fighter Wing at Bevecom, and it was SOC 17 October, 1956, and sold for scrap. MB-20 is seen here possibly at West Malling in June 1949 during exercise 'Bull Dog'. *(MAP.)*

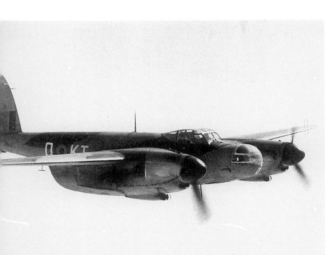

MB-11 seen here saw service as NT337 with No. 410 Squadron before entering BAF service in June 1948, first with No. 10 Squadron and then with the second Mosquito night-fighter squadron, No. 11 Squadron at Bevecom, which was formed on 1 July, 1951. It was sold for scrap in October 1956. These war-weary Mosquitoes became difficult to maintain and all except MB-24 were grounded in 1953 because of a fault in the engine mountings and excessive wear on the undercarriages; there were no funds available to the BAF for repair or replacement of these parts, and by October 1956 all aircraft had been SOC. *(Rudy Binnemans.)*

The BAF also bought seven T.IIIs plus another for ground instruction use, three FB.VIs and another kept in the UK to instruct Belgian personnel there, and one each of the NF.XVII (HK327) and NF.XIX (MM631), both for ground instructional use. Two T.IIIs are in this picture, with what appears to be MA-1 on the left. *(AELR via Mike Terlinden.)*

MB-24 (RK952) was delivered to the BAF in 1953, at the time all the other NF.30s were grounded, but MB-24 had already been modified and it soldiered on until 1956 with No. 10 Squadron, then at Beauvechain, but only on radar and beacon calibration flights and as a target aircraft for the Meteor NF.11s that had superseded the Mosquitoes. On 17 March, 1957, it was allocated to the Musée de l'Armée for preservation and in 1968 was repainted at Coxyde. It is seen here in the storage hall of the Musée de l'Armée in Brussels where it was photographed in July 1970 by the author. It remains in good condition and is complete except for some of the radar parts. *(Stuart Howe.)*

No. 60 Squadron, South African Air Force, received its first Mosquitoes in January 1943 at Castle Benito, Tripoli, flying PR sorties over North Africa. At the end of the year the squadron was at San Severo and early in 1944 received their first PR.XVIs and operated as far afield as Austria and the Balkans. The squadron stood down on the 15 July, 1945, and the squadron's crews flew ten Mosquitoes from Italy to Zwarkop in South Africa, where they saw further service, with '4802' seen here. *(SAAF.)*

The French Air Force acquired over 100 Mosquitoes, the majority of which were FB.VIs, but also PR.XVIs and NF.30s. French aircrew underwent a transition course on to the Mosquito at Cottesmore and Upper Heyford in November 1945, and the first FB.VI squadron was formed at Dijon in France the same month, GC 1/3 'Corse' (No. 1 Squadron, 3rd Wing). The FAF named their squadrons after French regions, for example 'Corse' or Corsica. During its use of the FB.VI, GC 1/3 'Corse' became GC 1/6 from November 1946 to July 1949, except for the first six months of 1947, when at short notice the squadron took their Mosquitoes to Indo-china, where it was simply known as the 'Corse' Squadron. Seen here in Indo-china is RF876 (the FAF continued to use the RAF serial) on 21 March, 1947. The ground crew had named the Mosquito 'Le Requin' in memory of another Mosquito that had crashed a month earlier. *(via J. J. Pettit.)*

Starting up the engines for a training flight at Rabat-Sale in Morocco is an NF.30 of GCN 1/31 'Lorraine'. The last NF.30 was withdrawn from service on 17 June, 1953, at Tours after having suffered a blown tyre. This was the end of the Mosquito in FAF service. *(via J. J. Pettit.)*

Another photograph taken in the early 1950s at Rabat-Sale of a rather well-used-looking NF.30 up on a tail trestle with its gun-bay doors open for servicing. *(via J. J. Pettit.)*

PX243 of GC 1/6 'Corse' suffered a starboard engine failure
after a dogfight with another Mosquito, and the pilot, Lt.
Cases, was obliged to make a wheel's-up landing near Tiffet in
Morocco. The recovery vehicles are seen approaching behind
the port wing and the Mosquito was transported back to
Rabat, where it was repaired and flown again. One other unit,
GC 2/6 'Normandie-Niemen', operated the FB.VI and also
operated out of Rabat from 1947 until the FB.VI was
withdrawn from FAF service in July 1949, with many finding
their way to Israel. (*via J. J. Petit.*)

A rather nice view of a PR.XVI of GR 1/20 'Lorraine' over the rugged North African countryside, most likely the Atlas Mountains in Morocco. This squadron formed on the PR.XVI at Dijon in 1945, moved to Agadir and Rabat and then finally to Tours from April 1952 to June 1953, when the Mosquitoes were withdrawn from service and sold to Israel or were scrapped. A number carried on in use as instructional airframes and for some years an example was preserved at an unknown location, possibly Nîmes in Provence, although the largest known component existing in France today is a rudder that is stored by the Musée de L'Air at Le Bourget. *(via Francis Bergese.)*

During the early stages of Israel's 1948 War of Independence the fledgling Israeli Air Force decided it needed a multi-role combat aircraft and that both the Beaufighter and the Mosquito were ideally suited for this task. The IAF finally concentrated on the Mosquito, which was more readily available. The first two Mosquitoes, NS811 and NS812, were purchased clandestinely in England, but one crashed *en route*, while the other, flown by ex-RAF pilot John Harvey, reached Israel in June 1948 and was based at Ramat David airfield. After the British arms embargo was lifted, a number of PR.XVIs and TR.33s were flown to Blackbushe for overhaul by Eagle Aviation and were delivered to Israel by Peter Nock of West London Air Charter between October 1954 and August 1955. The TR.33 in the ferry markings of 4x 3186 was previously TW238 and served with No. 811 and 790 Squadrons FAA until put into store in July 1951 and sold to R. A. Short on 23 July, 1953. It was delivered by Peter Nock to Israel on 27 November, 1954. *(Ron Cranham.)*

A formation of IAF FB.VIs in 1954 over Ramat David. Because of re-equipment with jets the Mosquito squadrons were disbanded in 1955 and were concentrated into one unit, which in turn was disbanded and its Mosquitoes put into store in June 1956. The Mosquitoes had given excellent service with the IAF and were very highly thought of, and when the Sinai (Suez) Campaign started in October, the Mosquitoes were reactivated and attacked the Egyptian concentrations, proving that they could carry more ordnance and were more reliable than their jet successors. Not one Mosquito was lost to enemy action. *(Lt. Col. F. D. Easterman.)*

In February 1951 a contract was signed with the French for 59 Mosquitoes at a price of US $5000 each for a stored and hangared Mosquito, $13,000 for a serviceable trainer and $200 for one regarded as scrap but useful for parts. They were overhauled at Châteaudun and the first four Mosquitoes were flown out in April 1951. The IAF operated five marks of Mosquito, the T.III, FB.VI, PR.XVI, NF.30 and TR.33. In this photograph an FB.VI is coming in to land at Ramat David on 19 August, 1954. *(Lt. Col. F. D. Easterman.)*

Ground crew about to open the gun doors to service the .303 machine guns of an IAF FB.VI in April 1956. The IAF ground crews, despite lack of technical support, became very proficient on the Mosquito, hence the serviceability rate was very high. *(Lt. Col. F. D. Easterman.)*

The IAF acquired a number of PR.XVIs from Britain and France and these were used to photograph Egyptian positions before and during the Sinai Campaig. Israel also attempted to obtain Mosquitoes in Canada, but due to intervention from the USA only one example was released, and this crashed *en route* in May 1951. The remains of a Mosquito exist today with the IAF Museum, and the author located the remains of a TR.33 in a Kibbutz, which was shipped to the UK in 1980 for use in a Mosquito rebuild by the Mosquito Aircraft Museum. After leaving IAF service a number of Mosquitoes were allocated for display in Kubbutzim. *(IAF.)*

Twenty-six B.XXs were received by the USAAF from Canadian
production and these were modified to photo-reconnaissance
configuration at the Bell Niagara Modification Centre at
Buffalo, New York, where they received the designation F-8.
They were bought for $110,000 each and 11 aircraft served with
No. 375 Servicing Squadron, Eighth Air Force, at Watton,
England, on operations and were later exchanged for PR.XVIs.
The remaining aircraft stayed in the USA, and previous to this a
number of other Mosquitoes had travelled south, including six
B.VIIs. In the forefront is B.XX 43-34934, ex-KB132, which
was returned to the RAF in 1944. *(Bell Aerospace.)*

A B.XX undergoing engine runs outside the Bell Modification Centre. As early as 1941 the Americans had taken an interest in the Mosquito and serious consideration was given to building them under licence in the USA, and the US military authorities and the Curtiss-Wright Corporation were given plans and data to study. The US Navy and Marines also wanted the Mosquito and were quite desperate to obtain examples, but hesitation plus technological and national prejudice prevented this at a time when the calibre of an aircraft like the Mosquito was sorely needed. *(Bell Aerospace.)*

Large-scale USAAF operation of the Mosquito started in February 1944, when the 25th Bomb Group, 8th Air Force, was re-equipped with PR.XVIs at Watton led by Col. Leon Gray: the Group was part of a Wing led by Brig. Gen. Elliott Roosevelt, son of the former President. Roosevelt had earlier flown a Mk IV for the USAAF in Algiers, North Africa, in No. 10 Mosquito Special Task Force on operations there. It was in fact the only Mosquito the unit had and it was highly prized. At Watton, the 25th BG consisted provisionally of the No. 802 Reconnaissance Group, but after regularization the group became the 25th Bombardment Group (Reconnaissance), consisting of the 652nd Bombardment Squadron (Heavy Reconnaissance), equipped with B.17s and B.24s, the 653rd Bombardment Squadron (Light, Reconnaissance) and the 654th Bombardment Squadron (Heavy, Special), equipped with the Mosquito PR.XVI. Over 70 PR.XVIs were allocated to the USAAF under a reverse Lend-lease agreement for use in Europe. Shown here is NS748 of the 653rd BS at Watton, Norfolk.

PR.XVI MM386 was delivered to the USAAF at Burton Wood straight from the factory on 4 May, 1944. The 654th Squadron not only carried out weather missions (known as 'Blue Stocking') but also missions codenamed 'Red Stocking'. For these missions the Mosquito's bomb bay was fitted out with an oxygen system for a third crew member, whose task it was to operate a device known as the 'Joan-Eleanor', a lightweight UHF transmitter. The operator would talk directly to the agent on the ground, recording the conversation on the wire recorder. This method was much simpler than using coded radio messages – a 20 minute contact could pass as much information as would otherwise have taken days by conventional radio transmissions. These Mosquitoes also carried OSS agents in their bomb bays, who were then dropped over Germany. *(via Thomas G. Fields.)*

Some USAAF Mosquitoes were used for experimental radar work by the 482nd Bomb Group at Alconbury. Six PR.XVIs were specially modified to test 'H2X', the American form of 'H2S', an air-to-ground radar used for target marking. NS538 seen here was the prototype. Note the heavily modified nose.

The only US fighter squadron to be equipped with the Mosquito was the 416 Night Fighter Squadron, which converted to the type from the Beaufighter at Pisa in Italy, in early December 1944. The first operational sortie was completed on the night of 17/18 December. The squadron had about 12 NF.30s and MM765 seen here was one of the first to be delivered; they were used mainly in the ground attack role until replaced by P-61s in June 1945. Note the rather wintry conditions. *(USAF Museum.)*

The Dominican Air Force ordered six FB.VIs and '301' is seen here during its delivery flight in July 1948 taking on fuel at USAF Narsarssuak in south-west Greenland. The roundel was red and blue with a white cross, with the fin flash in similar colours. *(Alan G. Harwin.)*

Mosquitoes equipped No. 333 (Norwegian) Squadron's 'B' Flight from May 1943, and with the termination of hostilities in Europe, the Flight was renumbered No. 334 (Norwegian) Squadron and flew to Norway, where they were based at Gardermoen, just north of Oslo. Their main task became mail-run services between the UK and Norway up to 21 November, 1945, when all Norwegian units were transferred from RAF control to the Royal Norwegian Air Force. Nine days later the squadron and its eight remaining aircraft were deactivated and kept on a maintenance basis only until June 1948. In the meantime ten more FB.VIs and three T.IIIs were ordered from Britain, the squadron was reactivated on 1 June and moved to Sola airfield on the west coast of Norway. All Norwegian Mosquitoes were equipped with rockets and FB.VI TA487 AV-F is seen here being loaded with training rounds at Sola. *(Tom Arheim.)*

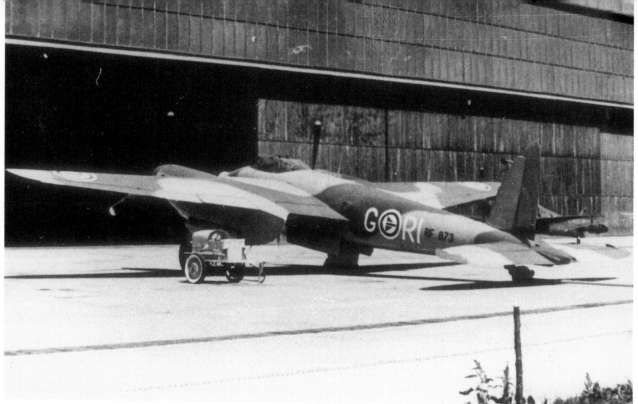

Two of the RNoAF FB.VIs were converted with airborne radar late in 1949 and early 1950, giving the aircraft a limited all-weather capability. One of them was RF873 shown here. The nose radar can just be seen. After a fatal accident in February 1951, when an aircraft lost both wings pulling up from a dive, all remaining Mosquitoes were grounded, and were finally struck off charge on 12 January, 1952. *(via Bjorn Olsen.)*

A single B.XXV also found its way into the Royal Norwegian Air Force inventory after being left behind by No. 162 Squadron, RAF, following an accident at Gardermoen in June 1945. With its engines removed it was transferred to the RNoAF Technical School at Kjevik and used for instructional purposes until it was scrapped in 1954. *(via Bjorn Olsen.)*

A fine study of No. 334 Squadron Mosquito FB.VI RS605,
which carries the incorrect serial number 'RS650', seen over the
Tyin Mountains in Southern Norway. It is piloted by Lt. Nilf
Arveschoug with Lt. Olav Kristian Fosen as his navigator during
a two-hour sortie for the benefit of Charles E. Brown. The
camera aircraft was a RNoAF Lodestar, RS605 was delivered
on 12 July, 1947 and was SOC in Norway on 12 January, 1952
with a total flying time of 493.45 hours.
(Charles E. Brown/RAF Museum.)

143

Undergoing minor maintenance on its starboard engine is 8114 (RF610), an FB.VI converted to T.III in Yugoslavia. After construction in September 1947, it was put into store for a few months until, in April 1948, it was allocated to the French Air Force. However, it remained in store and was instead issued to the Armament Practice Station at Acklington three months later and it remained there for over two years. After a further period in store it arrived in Yugoslavia on 5 September, 1952. Behind are several NF.38s, including 8052 (VX897), which are also undergoing routine servicing. *(Milan Micevski Collection.)*

In 1951 the 'Jugoslovensko ratno vazduhoplovstyo", or Yugoslav Air Force (JRV), visited Britain to negotiate for Mosquitoes under the Mutual Defence Aid Programme, and by the end of the year 33 had been delivered. In all the JRV received around 140 Mosquitoes, consisting of four T.IIIs, 76 FB.VIs and 50 NF.38s. The majority had not seen RAF service and were taken out of storage and delivered to Yugoslavia via No. 10 Ferry Unit at Abingdon. FB.VI 8117 (TA484), seen here before delivery, had been in store for over five years before being despatched on 22 July, 1952, to Yugoslavia, where it arrived the following day. The roundel later had a red star superimposed on it, as did the fin flash, the latter painted horizontally on the rudder after delivery. *(via R. C. Sturtivant.)*

The first JRV unit to convert to Mosquitoes was the 103rd Reconnaissance Regiment at Pančevo near Belgrade, which acted as a conversion centre for the other units due to receive the Mosquito; these were the 32nd Bomber Division (with FB.VIs) based in Zagreb, the 184th Reconnaissance Regiment (directly assigned to the 3rd Aviation Corps) and the 97th Aviation Regiment, which was part of the 21st Mixed Aviation Division for Navy support. In the spring of 1952 the JRV's Aviation Test Centre received one NF.38 and one FB.VI for research, testing and performance measuring. Here on the landing approach is 8137, ex-TA603, which was constructed late in 1945, spent 18 months with the Fighter Command Communications Squadron and then went into long-term storage with No. 38 MU, where it remained until it was delivered to Yugoslavia, via No. 10 Ferry Unit, on 1 November, 1952. *(Milan Micevski Collection.)*

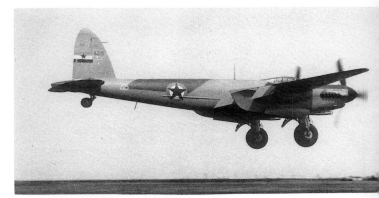

Just about to touch down is 8035 (VX903) of the 103rd Reconnaissance Regiment at Pančevo. In 1953 there were a number of border incidents with the Soviet Union and Hungary and JRV Mosquitoes made a number of sorties in these areas to help counter them. In March Mosquitoes escorted Marshal Tito's ship as he returned from the UK, but by September political relations between Yugoslavia and Italy were reaching their lowest ebb, because of an unresolved problem: 'Slobodna teritorija Trsta' (the Free Territory of Trieste). In early 1953 the Italian Army walked into the so-called Zone 'A' (city of Trieste) and on 8 October Yugoslavia decided to defend its own interests by putting her armed forces at their highest readiness and to enter Zone 'B'. The Mosquitoes of the 97th and 184th Aviation Regiments and the 32nd Bomber Division undertook reconnaissance and observation sorties in the border zone and in Italian air space, but before these dramatic events could explode into full-scale hostilities the two governments settled their problems peacefully. *(Milan Micevski Collection.)*

NF.38 8053 (VX907) of the 184th Reconnaissance Regiment sporting a white outboard wing, which signified that it belonged to the 'Aggressors'. The last operational Mosquito unit in the JRV was the 184th, which operated the type until the middle of 1960. Nine FB.VIs and two T.IIIs, however, formed a new sea-reconnaissance squadron which was used mainly in the target-tug role for the anti-aircraft school at Zadar. They were finally withdrawn from service in 1963, having given 12 years of very successful service. *(Milan Micevski Collection.)*

In October 1953, testing was undertaken with TR-45/A torpedoes mounted on FB.VIs. The torpedo bombing trials were successful, so in 1954 four FB.VIs of the 97th Aviation Regiment were converted to carry the TR-45/A torpedo, and one was loaded with the 'ASAG' minelaying system. In 1957 experiments were also carried out with the Yugoslav-built Letor-2 torpedo. In this photograph the torpedo is being mounted under the Mosquito's belly. Note also the faired-over cannon ports. *(Milan Micevski Collection.)*

Flown by Flt. Lt. Wool and his navigator Sgt. John Fielden, PR.IV DK310 of No. 1 PRU force-landed because of engine trouble at Berne-Belp airfield in Switzerland on 24 August, 1942. The crew were later released, but DK310 was sold to Switzerland on 3 July, 1944. Before this it was coded E-42 by the Swiss Army and was flown to Lucerne-Emmen to be evaluated by pilots of the 'Kriegstechnishe Abteilung' (KTA) on 6 September, 1943; the evaluation ended on 13 October, 1944. The Mosquito was then handed over to Swissair and given the civil registration HB-IMO for the purpose of training civil pilots to use her on night mail runs. This came to nothing and it returned to the KTA, recoded B-4, and when its flying career came to an end on 21 August, 1946, it had accumulated 39 hr 33 mins flying time in Switzerland.

FB.VI NS993 also force-landed in Switzerland and was officially recorded as missing on 30 September, 1944. It had previously served with Nos. 617 and 515 Squadrons. It was pressed into service by the KTA and was modified as a test bed for the Swiss SM-1 turbofan version of the Armstrong Siddeley Mamba, which was intended to power the Swiss-designed N-20 jet fighter. The SM-1 was housed in an aerofoil section and installed under the bomb bay of NS993, which had been given the Swiss code of B-5. After use, NS993, together with DK310, was stored in a hangar for a number of years before it was scrapped – not because of a hangar clear-out but because an officer thought he could smell glue deterioration, and fearing the Mosquitoes were about to disintegrate they were destroyed. Today, one of the Merlins and the cameras from DK310 are on display in the Swiss Air Force Museum at Dubendorf.

Civil Mosquitoes

Many surplus Mosquitoes were put on the civil registers of Britain and several overseas countries for several reasons, such as sales to an overseas government through an arms dealer, where the aircraft had first to be registered in Britain, test work, and for survey and mapping operations, for which the Mosquito was ideally suited. Others, especially in the USA, where the Mosquito's speed did not go unnoticed, were used for pylon racing and record breaking.

The first user of civil Mosquitoes was BOAC, which operated the type from 1943 until the war's end. In 1948 the BEA Gust Research Unit used two PR.34s for research into the problem of clear-air turbulance. In the late 1940s and early 1950s, a large number of Mosquitoes destined for Israel were put on the civil register. In 1963 a number of TT.35s and T.IIIs were purchased by Mirisch Films Ltd to star in the film *633 Squadron* and many of these aircraft are still in existence today.

Overseas, Spartan Air Services of Ottawa operated ten Mosquitoes and across the border in the USA the Mosquito was used for a wide variety of purposes, including racing, survey work and as a high-speed aircraft for drug trafficking. US-registered Mosquitoes were also used by the CIA for clandestine work outside the USA. Other examples appeared on the civil registers of Spain, Switzerland, Kenya, Argentina, Mexico, Australia and New Zealand. Today, only one Mosquito is currently on the civil register, US-Registered B.35 N35MK (RS712), owned and flown by Kermit Weeks.

Early in 1948 two Mosquitoes were allocated on loan to British European Airways to be used by their Gust Research Unit based at Cranfield. From there they flew all over Europe and Scandinavia investigating clear-air turbulence in readiness for the operation of the new Vickers Viscount at heights above 20,000ft. PR.34A G-AJZE (RG231) was allocated on 1 March, 1948, and PR.34A G-AJZF (RG238) on 9 June. Both aircraft were operated by BEA for two years and were returned to the RAF after overhaul by Marshalls at Cambridge, where they are seen in 1952. *(via Alan J. Wright.)*

The only other British post-war civil operator of the Mosquito was Flight Refuelling Ltd, who bought two NF.XIXs on 21 February, 1949, G-ALGU (TA299) and G-ALGV (TA343). Both were in store at No. 9 MU Cosford and 'LGU pictured here was flown to Tarrant Rushton on 3 March by Capt. Erington. After conversion its CofA was issued on 7 October, following an air test on 31 August, by pilot Hornidge, who made further air tests on 17 October and 29 December. Marian Kozubski flew 'LGU as a photo aircraft to film the Meteor link-ups with Lancaster tanker G-33-2 over Poole Harbour, Dorset. It was withdrawn from use in 1953, but 'LGV, after flying to Tarrant Rushton on 28 March, 1949, by Capt. Erington, was never converted and after being used as a source of spares for 'LGU was scrapped in 1952.
(via R. C. Sturtivant.)

N4928V was bought by Aviation Export Co of California in Australia and imported into the USA, where it was owned, along with two other US-registered Mosquitoes, by Richard Neuman. Subsequently they were used for a number of tasks, from smuggling auto parts to various South American countries to carrying out work for the CIA. N4928V was eventually scrapped at Burbank, California, along with N4935V, but Neuman removed the engines and all of the metal components, which he then stored, and these were recently acquired by Jim Merizan to aid him in his task of rebuilding several Mosquitoes. Note the Anson antenna attached to the canopy, while on the port side of the nose was painted, in large letters, 'PRESS ON REGARDLESS!' Photo taken at Mascot before departure.
(via D. A. S. MacKay and J. M. G. Graddidge.)

In 1941 the British Overseas Airways Corporation started operating a small-scale freight and mail service from Scotland to Sweden, but these operations were very hazardous and BOAC pleaded for Mosquitoes, which could outpace enemy fighters and fly above the flak. Eventually PR.IV DZ411 was allocated and was delivered to BOAC as G-AGFV on 15 December, 1942. It made its first flight from Leuchars to Stockholm on 4 February, 1943, crewed by Capt. C. B. Houlder and Radio Officer F. Frape. BOAC eventually operated a total of ten Mosquitoes, comprising the PR.IV and nine FB.VIs, but in addition three T.IIIs were loaned by the RAF for crew training. Besides freight and mail the Mosquitoes also carried engineering products and passengers in the bomb bay. From April 1943 to March 1945 these Mosquitoes flew 783,680 service miles and operations ended on 17 May, 1945. During the time four aircraft were lost. After over two years with BOAC, G-AGFV was returned to the RAF on 6 January, 1945, when it was put into store and was SOC on 10 October, 1946.
(British Aerospace.)

In December 1954 the Canadian aerial survey company Spartan Air Services purchased fifteen Mosquito B.35s. Ten were flown to Canada but five remained in the UK and were ferried to Hurn. Here, three were shipped to Canada (CF-IMA, 'IMC and 'IMD) while CF-IMB and 'IME remained at Hurn. CF-IMB here was ferried from store at Shawbury to Croydon on 15 August, 1955 by Marian Kozubski, and then to Hurn on 26 January, 1957. Both aircraft, seen here in 1962, were still in a fair condition. *(MAP.)*

The ten Spartan Mosquitoes were overhauled by Derby Aviation Ltd at Burnaston to civil standards and CF-HMN (TA713) was ferried to Canada by Peter Nock, departing Prestwick 11 September, 1955, flying via Keflavik, Sondrestrom, Goose and on to Spartan's Ottawa base where it arrived on the 14th. On *22 January, 1956, 'HMN was destroyed during a charter for a subsidiary of Standard Oil of New Jersey whilst photographing sites in Colombia. Its pilot, Al McNutt, put it down in a field near Bogotá. McNutt then flew back to Ottawa and returned a week later in another Mosquito to carry on the charter. *(A. J. Jones.)*

One of the Spartan Mosquitoes, CF-HMK, ended its days in Argentina as LV-HHN and in this photograph the starboard engine is receiving attention. CF-HMK started out as VR794, and like the other airworthy Spartan Mosquitoes was stored at No. 22 MU, Silloth, and authority to release VR794 was received on 22 November, 1954, with the aircraft being ferried to Derby Aviation by David Ogilvy, who also carried out its post-overhaul test flight on 19 May, 1955. Two days later Peter Nock departed Prestwick in 'HMK, arriving in Ottawa on the 23rd. The spare engines acquired by Spartan had in many cases somewhat suspect histories and engine failures were not uncommon; 'HMK suffered such a failure on 25 July, 1957, with a total time on the engine of only 210hr 55 min. By 20 April, 1961, airframe hours totalled 922hr 20 min. On 28 December it was registered in Argentina as LV-HHN to Servicios Aeroes Spartan SA. The pilot in Argentina was retired Navy officer Esteban Vigerti, the mechanic and co-pilot a civil employee of the Air Force. On 22 November, 1962, whilst flying at 7000 metres over San Luis, they encountered a problem with the port engine and decided to land at Rio Cuarto. Prior to landing, the Mosquito veered to the left and crashed, wrecking both undercarriages and damaging the fuselage. It was later sold. *(Dr. Atigo Marino.)*

One of the Spartan B.35s on an outing to the USA, seen here on 11 May, 1957, at Lambeth Field, St. Louis. CF-HMM (ex-TK623) reached Ottawa on 18 August, 1955, and as an indication of how hard these Mosquitoes worked, 'HMM flew 510 hours between May 1957 and March 1959; it too suffered an engine failure on 14 January, 1959. On 27 March, 1960, it was written off in a crash in the Dominican Republic. The Spartan Mosquitoes were modified to carry a third crew member, the camera operator, and were also given a new, clear nose cone and modified canopy. For additional range an extra bomb bay tank was fitted. In order to make room for the Swiss-built Wild RC-8 aerial camera, the fuselage bulkheads aft of the wing were moved and with the camera operating through a Perspex panel in the floor. The rear entry hatch was also modified for easier access for the camera operator. The Spartan Mosquitoes operated up to 35,000ft and were allowed by the Canadian Dept. of Transport to fly up to a maximum speed of 400 mph. A typical duration was 4½ hours, and these Mossies operated a survey work not only in Canada, the USA and South America but also South Africa. Three Spartan Mosquitoes survive today and two of these are being rebuilt to fly again. *(Dave Ostrowski.)*

B.25 N37878 (ex-KB377) was bought by Don McVicar in 1948, who had it registered as CF-FZG and entered it for the 1948 Bendix Trophy Race, but on the way to start the race it blew the starboard engine. It was then purchased by Don Bussart, who painted it blue overall with white lettering for the 1949 race. An hour out of Longbeach, California, he lost an engine, but he carried on and averaged a speed of over 300 mph for the course. Bussart later sold the aircraft to the Mark Hurd Aerial Survey Co, who later abandoned it at Las Vegas after a ground accident, when the air bottle for the pneumatic brakes over-filled and exploded, leaving a giant hole in the side of the fuselage. *(MAP.)*

In July 1956 B.35 TK655 was registered as G-AOSS to Derby Aviation Ltd, at Burneston, who started overhauling it for a 4500-mile South Atlantic record attempt by Miss Roberta Cowell, but the project was abandoned because of a lack of suitable engines and G-AOSS was scrapped in 1960. The author of this book has in his possession the airspeed indicator from this aircaft. It is seen here pushed out to grass at Burneston in the company of two derelict Ansons. *(Dave Welch.)*

After a brief period with the USAAF, PR.XVIs NS812 and NS811 were sold to Gp. Capt. Leonard Cheshire and registered to VIP Association Ltd at Cambridge as G-AIRT and G-AIRU respectively, and in May 1948 both were then sold on to dealer H. L. White. On 5 July, ferry pilot John Harvey collected 'IRT to take it to Exeter, but it never reached its destination. Harvey evaded air traffic control to take it out of the country to Israel, which at that time had an arms embargo in force. While over Southern France Harvey had to land at Nice to investigate a fuel problem and was detained by the French police. He was released and continued his journey via Corsica and Athens, but on reaching Israel's coastline his fuel gauges were down to zero, so he landed at Haifa airfield, still under nominal RAF control, where he was refuelled. He then continued his journey to the IAF's Ramat David airfield, where 'IRT became the first IAF Mosquito to enter service. 'IRU departed Abingdon to fly to Thame on 16 July and again evaded ATC, but crashed on landing at Ajaccio in Corsica; the pilot escaped unhurt. In the background is Horsa PF696, which arrived a month before 'IRT. *(via Alan J. Wright.)*

Two Mosquito PR.41s were entered for the speed section of the 1953 London to Christchurch air race, VH-KLG (ex-A52-324 and A52-62) and VH-WAD (ex-A52-319 and A52-210). VH-WAD's entry was cancelled because of financial problems and KLG was modified by DH at Bankstown with Merlin 77 engines, three-stage superchargers and long-range tanks in the bomb day. On its way to Britain, flown by Sqn. Ldr. A. J. R. Oates and Flt. Lt. D. H. Swain, KLG crashed on 3 October, when, following navigational problems, Oates crash-landed the Mosquito on a mud flat near Mergui in southern Burma; both men escaped unhurt. VH-WAD is currently being restored at Bankstown by the Australian War Memorial. *(via D. A. S. Mackay and J. M. G. Gradidge.)*

Another view of B.25 CF-FZG owned by Don McVicar taken before he sold it to Don Bussart when it became N37878. *(via Dick Hill.)*

PR.34 N9868F (ex-PF670) was one of five surplus Mosquitoes bought by Jack Amman Photogrammetric Engineers of San Antonio, Texas, on 16 October, 1956. They were converted for the survey role at Hatfield and while two left for the USA, the other three were flown to Libya to undertake a survey contract there. Peter Nock collected N9868F from Hatfield on 9 October, 1957, to fly to Stansted, on the way test flying the Mosquito to 30,000 ft. The same day he flew direct to Tripoli, a flight of 5½ hours duration. A month later one of Amman's British pilots flew the aircraft back to Cambridge. Peter Nock then left Cambridge on 5 November in N9868 for the USA via Prestwick, Iceland, Greenland and Canada, arriving in San Antonio on the 14th with a flying time of 27½ hours. After a further period of work it lay derelict at San Antonio along with a second Mosquito, N9871F (RG300). The photo was taken at Cambridge before its delivery to the USA.
(Aviation Photo News.)

XB-HOB is a Canadian-built Mosquito that was purchased by Luis Struck of Mexico City for use in aerial survey work in Mexico. It is seen here at Downsview before its delivery to Mexico. A second Mosquito was registered in Mexico, B.35 XB-TOX, ex-TA717, which was operated by Fotogramex SA in Mexico City and could well have been used as a source of spares for XB-HOB. The remains of XB-TOX were taken to Canada where they exist today. *(MAP.)*

FB.VI NX66422 was built at Hatfield late in 1944 as PZ467, and after a period in store was despatched to the USA on 9 April, 1945, for use by the US Navy, and it arrived at Patuxent River on 30 April; it became USN 91106. It was then used for tests involving the 57 mm Molins gun, was later sold as surplus and put on the American civil register as NX66422. It had two owners before being sold to Di Ponti Aviation of St. Paul, Minnesota who intended to enter it in the 1947 Bendix Trophy Race. This did not happen and it was sold to Mr Gene Doar, who planned to break Howard Hughes's around-the-world speed record. One Sunday he took the Mosquito up on a promotional flight from Charlotte and after several low passes he made a heavy landing and crashed on the runway. NX66422 is seen here painted silver overall with the name 'The Silver Streak' painted on its side, presumably after the time it was purchased by Mr Doar. The starboard engine appears to be receiving some attention. *(via R. C. Sturtivant.)*

FB.VI N9909F was built at Hatfield as PZ474 early in 1945, and after service with Nos 80 and 132 OCUs, and then a period of storage, was sold to New Zealand on 23 January, 1948. It left for New Zealand on 4 March piloted by P1. D. E. M. Atkins with W.O.I.M. Clarke and arrived on 3 April, in New Zealand where it was allocated the RNZAF serial NZ2384. It was put into storage at Taieri and, along with five others, was purchased by Aircraft Supplies of Palmerston North for an American customer, but when the New Zealand Government queried the ultimate destination the deal collapsed and only NZ2384, by then registered ZK-BCV on 2 September, 1953, was allowed to leave under contract for Trans World Engineering. Elgen Long flew the Mosquito out of Palmerston North on 10 March, 1955 via Nandi (11th), Canton Island (14th), Honolulu (16th) and arrived at San Francisco on 22 March. At the time Elgen was employed by 'Flying Tigers'. On arrival in the USA it was sold to the Insurance Finance Corporation of Studio City, California, and became N9909F. Its subsequent use is not clear, except that it was used for intelligence-gathering operations by the CIA in South America and was flown a number of times by Lewis Leach, Jr. It ended its days at Whiteman Air Park, San Fernando, California, and is here seen there in August 1957. The remains of this aircraft are now in the safe hands of James Merizan in California for restoration. *(John Brown.)*

B.25 N66313 'Miss Marta' (ex-KA984) was bought in June 1948 by Don McVicar of Montreal. It was sold to Jessie Stallings of Capitol Airways Inc., who raced it in the 1948 Bendix Trophy Race across the USA and took fifth place. Jesse Stallings, who was President of Capitol Airways, has high praise for the Mosquito, stating that its handling characteristics were as good as any aeroplane he had flown in 40 years. The aircraft is painted white overall with maroon engine cowlings and nacelles. It was later sold to the Mark Hurd Aerial Survey Co in California, but was written off when it ground looped on take-off in El Paso, Texas. *(Jesse Stallings.)*

Two more photographs of B.25 N37878 while with the Mark Hurd Aerial Survey Co. The front three-quarters view clearly shows the much modified entry hatch and was taken shortly before the accident which ended its flying career at Las Vegas. Although the damage was on the starboard side of the fuselage the side view was clearly taken after the accident, as debris can be seen hanging underneath the fuselage and there is some damage to the port side just behind the wing. *(J. D. R. Rawlings and Dave Ostrowski Collection.)*

B.25 N1203V, ex-KA997, was bought by Bob and Dianna Bixby for a new attempt on the round-the-world speed record, leaving San Francisco on 1 April 1950. They reached Cairo and flew on to Calcutta, but later had to abandon the attempt because of engine trouble. In 1954 Mrs Dianna Bixby planned a solo round-the-world record attempt, but weather and technical problems caused this to be cancelled. In this photograph the nose cone and side windows have been painted over and 'The Huntress', the name the Bixby's christened the aircraft, can clearly be seen. The colour scheme appears to be light grey and maroon. *(Dave Ostrowski Collection.)*

After plans for the round-the-world record attempt were abandoned, N1203V was extensively modified for high altitude work by Clair Waterbury. The entire forward fuselage was replaced with an all-metal one and Mustang Merlins were fitted. Waterbury sold the Mosquito to 'Flying Tigers' and it was flown by Jack Tallington, who flew most of the survey fights at 42,000 ft. It was eventually written off in Haiti in 1956, when its pilot ground looped the Mosquito on landing. In this picture N1203V wears a new colour scheme and shark's teeth insignia on the nose and underwing tanks. *(R. T. O'Dell.)*

Mosquito Miscellany

A nice angle of Spartan Air Services B.35 CF-HML (VR796). Note the modified escape hatch. Its last flight was from Lakehead to Uplands, Ottawa on 28 June, 1963 piloted by Vern Schille. By this time it had accumulated only 616.05 flying hours. *(George Hunter.)*

During its latter years with Spartan, the company used 'HML as a dual-control trainer, replacing FB.26 CF-GKK in this role. *(George Hunter.)*

Two more shots of the Flight Refuelling NF.XIXs,
G-ALGU (TA299) and G-ALGV (TA343) in late 1949.
Note the roughly painted-out RAF markings and the two
sizes of civil registrations. *(via Cobham PLC/C.Cruddas.)*

Of the five B.35s purchased by
Spartan in July 1955, three in the
form of CF-IMA, 'IMC and 'IMD
were dismantled and shipped to
Canada by sea for use as spares.
'IMD was ferried from 27 MU
Shawbury to Kidlington by Marian
Kozubrski on 13 August, 1955
ending up at Hurn (Bournemouth)
Airport where it is seen being
'dismantled' for shipment on 12
April, 1958. *(J.M.G.Gradidge.)*

Donald E.Bussart lining up in B.25 N37878 for the racehorse start of the 1949 Bendix Air Race at Rosamond Dry Lake, California. Don's hopes of winning the race were dashed when he lost the starboard engine, but he carried on with the port engine at full bore, finishing fourth at an average speed of 343.757mph.
(Don Bussart.)

Donald E. Bussart with his beloved 'Wooden Wonder' at Berry Field, Nashville in August 1949. It was there that Capital Airways prepared his Mosquito for the 1949 Bendix Air Race, a non-stop flight of 2008 miles from Rosamond, California to Cleveland on 2 September.
(Don Bussart.)

A pleasing study of B.25 NI203V, 'The Huntress', owned by Bob and Dianna Bixby.
(Brad Kemp via Mel Brown.)

FB.40 N4928V was purchased in Australia by Clair Waterbury from Morry Lawrence. The future N4928V (A52-177?) is the middle of the three Mosquitoes awaiting disposal at Forest Hill (Wagga Wagga) in 1953. After rebuilding, Waterbury was joined by Lewis Leach for the ferry flight to the USA but on the first leg to Mascot, Sydney one of the main legs failed to retract but fortunately did so for the landing! The first attempt to leave Australia was aborted due to compass failure – possibly due to the large amount of spares being carried, including a spare crankshaft in the nose! N4935V was also purchased in Australia and both aircraft were sold again in the USA, this time to Richard Neuman. (See page 150.)

Two other US registered Mosquitoes were purchased in Australia by Joe Mullen of Aero Service Corporation in May 1954, who had a contract with the US Army Map Service to photograph a section of Borneo from 36,000 feet. These were PR.41s N1596V (A52-197, A52-306 and VH-WWS) and N1597V (A52-204, A52-313 and VH-WWA). With modifications completed, RAAF test pilot W.M. (Max) Garroway took Joe Mullen on a height test to 36,000 feet on 30 May and soon after the two Mosquitoes departed for Borneo. They returned to Australia on 21 September and were stored at Camden. In May 1955, a team from the USA headed by Homer Jensen installed a magnetometer inside N1596V. The installation worked and Max headed for Broome in West Australia to do an oil search

for West Australian Petroleum over the Canning Desert, the job being completed on 3 September, 1955. It was used on another survey job in July 1956 and ended its days at Camden.
(Both Morry Lawrence.)

B.35 G-AOSS (TK655) at Burneston in 1957. (See page 153 for further details.) Derby Aviation were by this time well used to working on civil B.35s, having previously prepared the Spartan Mosquitoes. TK652 was also converted after being sold by R.K. Dundas Ltd to Capt.Rudi Bey of the Spanish airline Iberia. It was registered EC-WKH and Bey used it to commute between his home in Majorca to Madrid! Peter Nock flew it to Blackbushe on 7 July, 1956, then on the 13 July to Madrid via Bordeaux in a flying time of 3 hours 20 minutes. It eventually suffered an accident and was written off.

A familiar shot of Swiss-owned PR.IV DK310 in the civil marks of HB-IMO when it was briefly employed by Swissair. (See page 147.)

PR.34 RG300 of No. 58 Squadron at St. Eval in 1946 at the start of what was to become a long and eventful career (See page 93) in both military and civil guises. *(R.E.Hillard via Andrew Thomas.)*

RG300 was sold to Jack Ammann Photogrammetric Engineers of San Antonio, Texas as N9871F – one of five purchased in May 1956. After being retired from service in 1959 at San Antonio, it went through two further owners before being abandoned on the airfield.

A sad end for the faithful N9871F at San Antonio, its back broken and being picked over by souvenir hunters. The remains were rescued by the Confederate Air Force and later donated to Jim Merizan of California for use in his restoration projects. *(Mel Brown.)*

PR.41 A52-319 (also A52-210) first flew from Bankstown on 29 January, 1948 but never saw RAAF service and was placed into storage. It was eventually bought for £100 on 20 March, 1953 by Capt. James 'Jimmy' Woods, whose intention was to enter it into the 1953 London to Christchurch, New Zealand, Air Race and registered it as VH-WAD. Jimmy's sponsorship was withdrawn and VH-WAD lay derelict at Perth. In 1979 it was bought by the Australian War Memorial and has been fully restored by Hawker de Havilland at Bankstown.

Percival-built at Luton in September 1945, PR.34 PG623 was one of three such aircraft that supported the formation of six Vampires which crossed the Atlantic from Odiham to the USA, departing on 14 July, 1948 (further details on page 96c.) It is here being refuelled at Keflavik, Iceland.
(Alan G. Harwin)

PR.34a RG314 of No.81 Squadron at Seletar, Singapore about to depart on the last operational sortie of a Mosquito in RAF service on 15 December, 1955. (See page 88.)

Another shot of one of the PR.34s that supported the Vampires, this time PF621 at Goose Bay, Labrador undergoing an engine inspection. The Mossies were led by Squadron Leader H.B.Martin.
(Alan G. Harwin.)

B.35 RV340 of No. 98 Squadron at Melsbroek in Belgium having its compass swung. *(via Dillip Sarker.)*

A sad line-up of B.35s awaiting their fates in a Midland scrap yard.

This Mossie, barely recognisable as such, never saw active service. Instead B.XVI PF498 was delivered to RAF Kirkham and was given the instructional airframe number 6607M. On 6 June, 1955 it was allocated to the Civil Defence Unit at the Royal Ordnance Factory, Chorley, Lancashire for use in crash rescue training. PF498 refused to give up and in 1972 the wing was rescued by Tony Agar for possible use in his own Mosquito rebuild. (See page 36 for a service shot of PF498.)

Displayed at Lewis's Oxford Street store on 5 September, 1945 is what appears to be a factory-fresh B.35. It was part of a display entitled 'Britain's Aircraft Exhibition'. Note the 4000lb bomb and the rear fuselage section behind the starboard nacelle. Also, there appears to be a bomb carrier under the port wing. *(British Aerospace.)*

B.35s in the Airspeed, Portsmouth, fitting-out hangar late in 1947. The near aircraft, VR974, was sold to Spartan Air Services on 16 December, 1954 and became CF-HMK. *(British Aerospace.)*

TT.35 VP191 somewhat in the woods at Weston-Super-Mare on 17 July, 1962. Harry Ellis, Chief Pilot of No.3 CAACU at Exeter was just short of becoming airborne when he lost power in the starboard engine, finishing up in the trees just short of the railway embankment! *(via Harry Ellis.)*

Hatfield-built B.35 TH988 pictured at the 1953 Royal Aeronautical Society Garden Party at Hatfield. At this time it was engaged in guided missile research and was later converted to a target tug. Note the painted-over nose cone with what appears to be a scanner installed in the front. Also the pod mounted into the bomb bay and the padlock on the crew entry door for security! *(D.S. Skeggs.)*

While delivering a Canadian-built B.XX to Britain, Wing Commander John Wooldridge created a record for the fastest Atlantic crossing, flying from Labrador to Prestwick, coast-to-coast in 5 hours 40 minutes in May 1944. Take-off to landing was completed in 6 hours 40 minutes, a distance of 2200 miles. The navigator was F/O C.J.Bown. The Mosquito is seen here on display, probably at Hatfield. Wooldridge commanded No. 105 Squadron and was a great exponent of the Mosquito.

B.XXV KA970, on a delivery flight from Canada on 17 April, 1945, was the subject of an accident when an air bottle in the starboard side of the fuselage exploded some 75 miles from Prestwick. The pilot heard a loud explosion and his feet were knocked from the rudder pedals. The starboard engine had to be feathered and a belly landing followed.

The extent of the fuselage damage to KA970, seen here at Hatfield awaiting repair, is plain to see. Nos 3 and 4 bulkheads were severed for about 12ins of their circumference, No.5 was torn in half, No. 6 bulkhead and rudder lever distorted and the hydraulic tank smashed – yet it survived! The fuselage strengthener looks like it may have helped prevent even further damage. The toughness of the Mossie was one of the features that endeared it to its crews. *(British Aerospace.)*

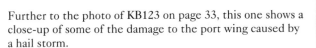

Further to the photo of KB123 on page 33, this one shows a close-up of some of the damage to the port wing caused by a hail storm.

In addition to the normal position for serial numbers on both sides of the rear fuselage, the FB. VIs of No. 45 Squadron also had it stencilled on the fin. The reason for this is unknown. The little figure painted on top of the rudder depicts a person blowing raspberries at the following aircraft! At this time the squadron was based at St. Thomaas Mount, Madras in India.
(Peter Sorrel via Peter Jolly).

A No. 84 Squadron FB.VI, RF726, near its Java base in March 1946, piloted by F/O A.B.Johnson with P/O P.H. Jenkins as navigator.

The crew entry hatch on the FB.VI was ideal for nose-art, this aircraft being the mount of an American pilot serving in No.82 Squadron in Burma early in 1945.
(Vic Hughes.)

A light-hearted group of airmen of No.55 Squadron at Hassani in Greece in the late summer of 1946. Wing Commander Donovan is swinging from the gun barrels! On top of the aircraft are a couple of pet dogs, which were quite common on RAF squadrons. No. 55 Squadron had a very short existence, being formed in July 1946 and disbanded on 1 November.

Walking down the Mosquito production line on 19 April, 1943, is the Rt. Hon. Winston Churchill, Prime Minister, accompanied by Capt. de Havilland on his right with A.S. Butler and Sir Stafford Cripps. Churchill had just been watching a demonstration of the secret Gloster E28/40, Mosquito and Tempest.

The last B.35 to be produced at Hatfield? The production workers pose by the fuselage which has signatures and slogans adorned all over it!

Mosquito wing spars leaving on a Ministry of Aircraft Production transporter, freshly made by Dancer & Hearne of High Wycombe. *(A.T. Emery.)*

Also at Dancer & Hearne, the ladies are putting the finishing touches to Mosquito fins. *(A.T. Emery.)*

F.II DD630 was constructed at Hatfield in the summer of 1942. Although perhaps not the usual practice in the RAF for outside servicing, indoor space was at a premium at Hatfield, so tents were erected on the grass to cover a Mosquito while work was carried out on it.

On the night of 24/25 March, 1944, F/O E.R.Hedgecoe of No. 85 Squadron shot down a Ju 188 over the sea in his NF.XII which exploded and showered the Mosquito with burning fuel. He was temporarily blinded and virtually all of the fabric covering from the aircraft was scorched and the canopy blackened. Hedgecoe later joined the Fighter Interception Unit and here destroyed a Ju 88, three Bf 110s and damaged three more. The Unit operated the Mosquito for trials and operational purposes, such as installing new radar equipment and experimental night patrols.

T.III VA883 of No. 609 Squadron at Yeadon in April 1947. The squadron code letters appear to be dark blue, outlined in yellow. *(Alan G.Harwin.)*

Chester-built TR.37 NT724 awaiting delivery. The TR.37 was similar to the TR.33 with updated radar and a range of 1100 miles on its internal tanks. The pneumatic undercarriage legs clearly visible here were installed on the Sea Mosquito principly to allow it to land on the deck of an aircraft carrier – if the normal rubber-in-compression legs were used, the aircraft would bounce off the flight deck due to the hard landings required! *(via Francis Bergese.)*

A rather nice study of a pair of NF.36s awaiting instructions to take-off in September 1948, possibly of No. 141 Squadron at Coltishall. The lead Mossie is RL176.

A pair of PR.XVIs of the French Air Force off the North
African coast, probably Algeria. *(via Francis Bergese.)*

Line-up of 32nd Bomber Division FB.VIs at Zagreb. The
Yugoslav Air Force received 140 Mosquitoes from Britain,
deliveries starting in 1951. They served quite successfully
for some 12 years. *(Milan Micevski Collection.)*

103rd Recce Regiment personnel 'hide' one of their NF.38s on a Yugoslavian air base in 1954. *(Milan Micevski Collection.)*

An Israeli Air Force Force FB.VI warming up, most likely at Ramat David circa 1954. Probably ex-French Air Force as the Israeli Air Force received some 60 Mosquitoes from this source plus further examples for use as spares. The Israelis thought very highly of the Mosquito.

FB.VI '302' of the Dominican Air Force, one of two that staged into USAF Narsarssuak, Greenland in July 1948 to take on fuel. Note the four-bladed propellers. *(Alan G. Harwin.)*

A number of Canadian B.XXs (F-8s) served with the
USAAF in Britain but were later swapped for PR.XVIs.
These B.XXs were passed to the RAF and, after overhaul,
gave good service in Bomber Command. Shown here is
334926 which was brought back to the UK by Hatfield test
pilot Pat Fillingham. The location is most likely Watton.

Chinese Air Force T.29 'T-97' (ex-
KA222) after its prang at Hankow
piloted by Canadian instructor
Johnny Turnbull. He is standing on
the cause of his prang – a blown tyre.
Of the large number of Mosquitoes
shipped to China only one exists
today, in the Chinese Air Force
Museum, although a good part of this
one appears to be replicated using a
bit of license! *(George Stewart.)*

A USAAF PR.XVI flying
over the English
countryside complete
with invasion stripes.